MANDALA SYMBOLISM

from

The Collected Works of C. G. Jung

VOLUME 9, PART I

BOLLINGEN SERIES XX

Mandala of a Modern Man

MANDALA
SYMBOLISM

C. G. JUNG

TRANSLATED BY R. F. C. HULL

BOLLINGEN SERIES

PRINCETON UNIVERSITY PRESS

First Princeton/Bollingen Paperback Edition, 1972
Third printing, 1973

Extracted from *The Archetypes and the Collective Unconscious*, Vol. 9, Part I, of the *Collected Works of C. G. Jung*. All the volumes comprising the *Collected Works* constitute number XX in Bollingen Series, under the editorship of Herbert Read (d. 1968), Michael Fordham, and Gerhard Adler; executive editor, William McGuire.

- LC Card 74-39057

ISBN 0-691-01781-6

Printed in the USA

EDITORIAL PREFACE

In his *Memories, Dreams, Reflections*, Jung tells of how he painted the first mandala, in 1916, after writing the "Seven Sermons to the Dead."[1] But it was not until 1918–19, when Jung was commandant of a British war prisoners' camp in French Switzerland, that he began to understand mandala drawings. "I sketched every morning in a notebook a small circular drawing, a mandala, which seemed to correspond to my inner situation at the time. With the help of these drawings I could observe my psychic transformations from day to day. . . . Only gradually did I discover what the mandala really is: 'Formation, Transformation, Eternal Mind's eternal re-creation' (*Faust, II*). And that is the self, the wholeness of the personality, which if all goes well is harmonious, but which cannot tolerate self-deceptions. My mandalas were cryptograms . . . in which I saw the self—that is, my whole being—actively at work. To be sure, at first I could only dimly understand them; but they seemed to me highly significant, and I guarded them like precious pearls. I had the distinct feeling that they were something central, and in time I acquired through them a living conception of the self. The self, I thought, was like the monad which I am, and which is my world. The mandala represents this monad, and corresponds to the microcosmic nature of the psyche."

Indeed, Jung's discovery of the mandala provided the key to his entire system. "I had to abandon the idea of the superordinate position of the ego. . . . I had to let myself be carried along by the current, without a notion of where it would lead me. When I began drawing the mandalas, however, I saw that everything, all the paths I had been following, all the steps I had taken, were leading back to a single point—namely, to the mid-point. It became increasingly plain to me that the mandala is the centre. It is the exponent of all paths. It is the path to the centre, to individuation.

"During those years, between 1918 and 1920, I began to understand that the goal of psychic development is the self. There is no linear evolution; there is only a circumambulation of the self. . . . This insight gave me stability, and gradually my inner peace returned. I knew that in finding the mandala as an expression of the self I had attained what was for me the ultimate."

1 *Memories, Dreams, Reflections* by C. G. Jung, recorded and edited by Aniela Jaffé, trans. Richard and Clara Winston (New York: Pantheon Books, 1963), pp. 195ff., including the quotations that follow. The Vintage edn. contains "Septem Sermones ad Mortuos" in an appendix. Jung's 1916 mandala is given as a frontispiece to the present volume.

Jung continued to study and to paint mandalas, but he did not publish any of them or present his conclusions about their significance, particularly in connection with the analytical technique he calls "active imagination," until 1929, in his commentary on Richard Wilhelm's translation of "The Secret of the Golden Flower." Among the mandala paintings given as illustrations were three by Jung, though they were acknowledged to be his only in *Memories, Dreams, Reflections*, published after his death.[2]

Mandala forms had fascinated Jung from the beginning of his career. In his M.D. dissertation, "On the Psychology and Pathology of So-called Occult Phenomena" (1902), his somnambulistic patient produced, in fantasy, a detailed circular diagram (the "circles of matter"; see *Coll. Works*, vol. 1, par. 65). In *Wandlungen und Symbole der Libido* (1911–12), which Jung wrote while he was working with Freud, he dwells on symmetrical dream-cities, crosses, sun-wheels, and mystic roses, though he did not identify these as mandala symbols until he revised the work in 1952 (*Coll. Works*, vol. 5).

In one of his last works, "Flying Saucers: A Modern Myth," written when Jung was in his eighties, he showed that the mandala is the pre-eminent symbol for our own time. "The psychological experience that is associated with the Ufo consists in the vision of the *rotundum*, the symbol of wholeness and the archetype that expresses itself in mandala form. Mandalas usually appear in situations of psychic confusion and perplexity. The archetype thereby constellated represents a pattern of order which, like a psychological 'view-finder' marked with a cross or a circle divided into four, is superimposed on the psychic chaos so that each content falls into place and the weltering confusion is held together by the protective circle" (*Coll. Works*, vol. 10, par. 803).

*

The present volume contains two important papers on mandala symbolism, with many illustrations, and a useful popular summary of the subject. In addition to the other writings mentioned in this preface, there is a significant treatment of the mandala in dream symbolism published as Part II of *Psychology and Alchemy* (*Coll. Works*, vol. 12).

[2] These three mandala paintings by Jung, and a fourth, are reproduced in the present volume as Figs. 6, 28, 29, and 36.

TABLE OF CONTENTS

LIST OF ILLUSTRATIONS

Mandala of a Modern Man   *frontispiece*

Painting by C. G. Jung, 1916. The microcosmic enclosed within the macrocosmic system of opposites. Macrocosm, top: boy in the winged egg, Erikapaios or Phanes, the spiritual principle with triadic fire-symbol and attributes; bottom, his dark adversary Abraxas, ruler of the physical world, with double pentadic star of natural man and rebirth symbols. Microcosm, left: snake with phallus, the procreative principle; right, dove of Holy Ghost with double beaker of Sophia. Inner sun (jagged circle) encloses repetitions of this system on a diminishing scale, with inner microcosm at the centre. (From *Du*, Zurich, April 1955, where the mandala was reproduced. Cf. *Memories, Dreams, Reflections*, p. 195, U.S.; 187, Brit.)

ix

MANDALA SYMBOLISM

MANDALAS [1]

713   The Sanskrit word *mandala* means "circle" in the ordinary sense of the word. In the sphere of religious practices and in psychology it denotes circular images, which are drawn, painted, modelled, or danced. Plastic structures of this kind are to be found, for instance, in Tibetan Buddhism, and as dance figures these circular patterns occur also in Dervish monasteries. As psychological phenomena they appear spontaneously in dreams, in certain states of conflict, and in cases of schizophrenia. Very frequently they contain a quaternity or a multiple of four, in the form of a cross, a star, a square, an octagon, etc. In alchemy we encounter this motif in the form of *quadratura circuli*.

714   In Tibetan Buddhism the figure has the significance of a ritual instrument (*yantra*), whose purpose is to assist meditation and concentration. Its meaning in alchemy is somewhat similar, inasmuch as it represents the synthesis of the four elements which are forever tending to fall apart. Its spontaneous occurrence in modern individuals enables psychological research to make a closer investigation into its functional meaning. As a rule a mandala occurs in conditions of psychic dissociation or disorientation, for instance in the case of children between the ages of eight and eleven whose parents are about to be divorced, or in adults who, as the result of a neurosis and its treatment, are confronted with the problem of opposites in human nature and are consequently disoriented; or again in schizophrenics whose view of the world has become confused, owing to the invasion of incomprehensible contents from the unconscious. In such cases it is easy to see how the severe pattern imposed by a

1 [Written especially for *Du: Schweizerische Monatsschrift* (Zurich), XV:4 (April 1955), 16, 21, and subscribed "January 1955." The issue was devoted to the Eranos conferences at Ascona, Switzerland, and the work of C. G. Jung. (An anonymous translation into English accompanying the article has been consulted.) With Dr. Jung's article also were several examples of mandalas, including the frontispiece of this volume and fig. 1, p. 13. While this brief article duplicates some material given elsewhere in this volume, it is presented here as a concise popular statement on the subject.—EDITORS.]

circular image of this kind compensates the disorder and confusion of the psychic state—namely, through the construction of a central point to which everything is related, or by a concentric arrangement of the disordered multiplicity and of contradictory and irreconcilable elements. This is evidently an *attempt at self-healing* on the part of Nature, which does not spring from conscious reflection but from an instinctive impulse. Here, as comparative research has shown, a fundamental schema is made use of, an archetype which, so to speak, occurs everywhere and by no means owes its individual existence to tradition, any more than the instincts would need to be transmitted in that way. Instincts are given in the case of every newborn individual and belong to the inalienable stock of those qualities which characterize a species. What psychology designates as archetype is really a particular, frequently occurring, formal aspect of instinct, and is just as much an *a priori* factor as the latter. Therefore, despite external differences, we find a fundamental conformity in mandalas regardless of their origin in time and space.

715   The "squaring of the circle" is one of the many archetypal motifs which form the basic patterns of our dreams and fantasies. But it is distinguished by the fact that it is one of the most important of them from the functional point of view. Indeed, it could even be called the *archetype of wholeness*. Because of this significance, the "quaternity of the One" is the schema for all images of God, as depicted in the visions of Ezekiel, Daniel, and Enoch, and as the representation of Horus with his four sons also shows. The latter suggests an interesting differentiation, inasmuch as there are occasionally representations in which three of the sons have animals' heads and only one a human head, in keeping with the Old Testament visions as well as with the emblems of the seraphim which were transferred to the evangelists, and—last but not least—with the nature of the Gospels themselves: three of which are synoptic and one "Gnostic." Here I must add that, ever since the opening of Plato's *Timaeus* ("One, two, three . . . but where, my dear Socrates, is the fourth?") and right up to the Cabiri scene in *Faust,* the motif of four as three and one was the ever-recurring preoccupation of alchemy.

716   The profound significance of the quaternity with its singular process of differentiation extending over the centuries, and now manifest in the latest development of the Christian symbol,[2]

[2] [Proclamation of the dogma of the Assumption of the Virgin, in 1950. Cf. *Psychology and Religion: West and East,* pars. 119ff., 251f., 748ff.—EDITORS.]

may explain why *Du* chose just the archetype of wholeness as an example of symbol formation. For, just as this symbol claims a central position in the historical documents, individually too it has an outstanding significance. As is to be expected, individual mandalas display an enormous variety. The overwhelming majority are characterized by the circle and the quaternity. In a few, however, the three or the five predominates, for which there are usually special reasons.

717   Whereas ritual mandalas always display a definite style and a limited number of typical motifs as their content, individual mandalas make use of a well-nigh unlimited wealth of motifs and symbolic allusions, from which it can easily be seen that they are endeavouring to express either the totality of the individual in his inner or outer experience of the world, or its essential point of reference. Their object is the *self* in contradistinction to the *ego*, which is only the point of reference for consciousness, whereas the self comprises the totality of the psyche altogether, i.e., conscious *and* unconscious. It is therefore not unusual for individual mandalas to display a division into a light and a dark half, together with their typical symbols. An historical example of this kind is Jakob Böhme's mandala, in his treatise *XL Questions concerning the Soule*. It is at the same time an image of God and is designated as such. This is not a matter of chance, for Indian philosophy, which developed the idea of the self, Atman or Purusha, to the highest degree, makes no distinction in principle between the human essence and the divine. Correspondingly, in the Western mandala, the *scintilla* or soul-spark, the innermost divine essence of man, is characterized by symbols which can just as well express a God-image, namely the image of Deity unfolding in the world, in nature, and in man.

718   The fact that images of this kind have under certain circumstances a considerable therapeutic effect on their authors is empirically proved and also readily understandable, in that they often represent very bold attempts to see and put together apparently irreconcilable opposites and bridge over apparently hopeless splits. Even the mere attempt in this direction usually has a healing effect, but only when it is done spontaneously. Nothing can be expected from an artificial repetition or a deliberate imitation of such images.

A STUDY IN THE PROCESS OF INDIVIDUATION [1]

> Tao's working of things is vague and obscure.
> Obscure! Oh vague!
> In it are images.
> Vague! Oh obscure!
> In it are things.
> Profound! Oh dark indeed!
> In it is seed.
> Its seed is very truth.
> In it is trustworthiness.
> From the earliest Beginning until today
> Its name is not lacking
> By which to fathom the Beginning of all things.
> How do I know it is the Beginning of all things?
> Through it!
>
> LAO-TZU, *Tao Teh Ching,* ch. 21.

Introductory

525   During the 1920's, I made the acquaintance in America of a lady with an academic education—we will call her Miss X—who had studied psychology for nine years. She had read all the more recent literature in this field. In 1928, at the age of fifty-five, she came to Europe in order to continue her studies under my guidance. As the daughter of an exceptional father she had varied interests, was extremely cultured, and possessed a lively turn of mind. She was unmarried, but lived with the unconscious equivalent of a human partner, namely the animus (the personification of everything masculine in a woman), in that

---

1 [Translated from "Zur Empirie des Individuationsprozesses," *Gestaltungen des Unbewussten* (Zurich, 1950), where it carries the author's note that it is a "thoroughly revised and enlarged version of the lecture of the same title first published in the *Eranos-Jahrbuch 1933*," i.e., in 1934. The original version was translated by Stanley Dell and published in *The Integration of the Personality* (New York, 1939; London, 1940). The motto by Lao-tzu is from a translation by Carol Baumann in her article "Time and Tao," *Spring,* 1951, p. 30.—EDITORS.]

characteristic liaison so often met with in women with an academic education. As frequently happens, this development of hers was based on a positive father complex: she was "fille à papa" and consequently did not have a good relation to her mother. Her animus was not of the kind to give her cranky ideas. She was protected from this by her natural intelligence and by a remarkable readiness to tolerate the opinions of other people. This good quality, by no means to be expected in the presence of an animus, had, in conjunction with some difficult experiences that could not be avoided, enabled her to realize that she had reached a limit and "got stuck," and this made it urgently necessary for her to look round for ways that might lead her out of the impasse. That was one of the reasons for her trip to Europe. Associated with this there was another—not accidental—motive. On her mother's side she was of Scandinavian descent. Since her relation to her mother left very much to be desired, as she herself clearly realized, the feeling had gradually grown up in her that this side of her nature might have developed differently if only the relation to her mother had given it a chance. In deciding to go to Europe she was conscious that she was turning back to her own origins and was setting out to reactivate a portion of her childhood that was bound up with the mother. Before coming to Zurich she had gone back to Denmark, her mother's country. There the thing that affected her most was the landscape, and unexpectedly there came over her the desire to paint—above all, landscape motifs. Till then she had noticed no such aesthetic inclinations in herself, also she lacked the ability to paint or draw. She tried her hand at watercolours, and her modest landscapes filled her with a strange feeling of contentment. Painting them, she told me, seemed to fill her with new life. Arriving in Zurich, she continued her painting efforts, and on the day before she came to me for the first time she began another landscape—this time from memory. While she was working on it, a fantasy-image suddenly thrust itself between her and the picture: she saw herself with the lower half of her body in the earth, stuck fast in a block of rock. The region round about was a beach strewn with boulders. In the background was the sea. She felt caught and helpless. Then she suddenly saw me in the guise of a medieval sorcerer. She shouted for help, I came along and touched the rock with

7

a magic wand. The stone instantly burst open, and she stepped out uninjured. She then painted this fantasy-image instead of the landscape and brought it to me on the following day.

Picture 1

526   As usually happens with beginners and people with no skill of hand, the drawing of the picture cost her considerable difficulties. In such cases it is very easy for the unconscious to slip its subliminal images into the painting. Thus it came about that the big boulders would not appear on the paper in their real form but took on unexpected shapes. They looked, some of them, like hardboiled eggs cut in two, with the yolk in the middle. Others were like pointed pyramids. It was in one of these that Miss X was stuck. Her hair, blown out behind her, and the movement of the sea suggested a strong wind.

527   The picture shows first of all her imprisoned state, but not yet the act of liberation. So it was there that she was attached to the earth, in the land of her mother. Psychologically this state means being caught in the unconscious. Her inadequate relation to her mother had left behind something dark and in need of development. Since she succumbed to the magic of her motherland and tried to express this by painting, it is obvious that she is still stuck with half her body in Mother Earth: that is, she is still partly identical with the mother and, what is more, through that part of the body which contains just that secret of the mother which she had never inquired into.

528   Since Miss X had discovered all by herself the method of active imagination I have long been accustomed to use, I was able to approach the problem at just the point indicated by the picture: she is caught in the unconscious and expects magical help from me, as from a sorcerer. And since her psychological knowledge had made her completely *au fait* with certain possible interpretations, there was no need of even an understanding wink to bring to light the apparent *sous-entendu* of the liberating magician's wand. The sexual symbolism, which for many naïve minds is of such capital importance, was no discovery for her. She was far enough advanced to know that explanations of this kind, however true they might be in other respects, had no significance in her case. She did not want to know how liberation might be possible in a *general* way, but

8

how and in what way it could come about for *her*. And about this I knew as little as she. I know that such solutions can only come about in an individual way that cannot be foreseen. One cannot think up ways and means artificially, let alone know them in advance, for such knowledge is merely collective, based on average experience, and can therefore be completely inadequate, indeed absolutely wrong, in individual cases. And when, on top of that, we consider the patient's age, we would do well to abandon from the start any attempt to apply ready-made solutions and warmed-up generalities of which the patient knows just as much as the doctor. Long experience has taught me not to know anything in advance and not to know better, but to let the unconscious take precedence. Our instincts have ridden so infinitely many times, unharmed, over the problems that arise at this stage of life that we may be sure the transformation processes which make the transition possible have long been prepared in the unconscious and are only waiting to be released.

529   I had already seen from her previous history how the unconscious made use of the patient's inability to draw in order to insinuate its own suggestions. I had not overlooked the fact that the boulders had surreptitiously transformed themselves into *eggs*. The egg is a germ of life with a lofty symbolical significance. It is not just a cosmogonic symbol—it is also a "philosophical" one. As the former it is the Orphic egg, the world's beginning; as the latter, the philosophical egg of the medieval natural philosophers, the vessel from which, at the end of the *opus alchymicum*, the homunculus emerges, that is, the Anthropos, the spiritual, inner and complete man, who in Chinese alchemy is called the *chen-yen* (literally, "perfect man").[2]

530   From this hint, therefore, I could already see what solution the unconscious had in mind, namely individuation, for this is the transformation process that loosens the attachment to the unconscious. It is a definitive solution, for which all other ways serve as auxiliaries and temporary makeshifts. This knowledge, which for the time being I kept to myself, bade me act with caution. I therefore advised Miss X not to let it go at a mere fantasy-image of the act of liberation, but to try to make a

2 Cf. *Psychology and Alchemy*, pars. 138f., 306, and Wei Po-yang, "An Ancient Chinese Treatise on Alchemy."

9

picture of it. How this would turn out I could not guess, and that was a good thing, because otherwise I might have put Miss X on the wrong track from sheer helpfulness. She found this task terribly difficult owing to her artistic inhibitions. So I counselled her to content herself with what was possible and to use her fantasy for the purpose of circumventing technical difficulties. The object of this advice was to introduce as much fantasy as possible into the picture, for in that way the unconscious has the best chance of revealing its contents. I also advised her not to be afraid of bright colours, for I knew from experience that vivid colours seem to attract the unconscious. Thereupon, a new picture arose.

Picture 2

531   Again there are boulders, the round and pointed forms; but the round ones are no longer eggs, they are complete circles, and the pointed ones are tipped with golden light. One of the round forms has been blasted out of its place by a golden flash of lightning. The magician and magic wand are no longer there. The personal relationship to me seems to have ceased: the picture shows an impersonal natural process.

532   While Miss X was painting this picture she made all sorts of discoveries. Above all, she had no notion of what picture she was going to paint. She tried to reimagine the initial situation; the rocky shore and the sea are proof of this. But the eggs turned into abstract spheres or circles, and the magician's touch became a flash of lightning cutting through her unconscious state. With this transformation she had rediscovered the historical synonym of the philosophical egg, namely the *rotundum,* the round, original form of the Anthropos (or στοιχεῖον στρογγύλον, 'round element,' as Zosimos calls it). This is an idea that has been associated with the Anthropos since ancient times.[3] The soul, too, according to tradition, has a round form. As the Monk of Heisterbach says, it is not only "like to the sphere of the moon, but is furnished on all sides with eyes" (*ex omni parte oculata*). We shall come back to this motif of polyophthalmia later on. His remark refers in all probability to certain parapsychological phenomena, the "globes of light" or globular

3 *Psychology and Alchemy,* par. 109, n. 38.

luminosities which, with remarkable consistency, are regarded as "souls" in the remotest parts of the world.[4]

533 The liberating flash of lightning is a symbol also used by Paracelsus [5] and the alchemists for the same thing. Moses' rock-splitting staff, which struck forth the living water and afterwards changed into a serpent, may have been an unconscious echo in the background.[6] Lightning signifies a sudden, unexpected, and overpowering change of psychic condition.[7]

534 "In this Spirit of the Fire-flash consists the Great Almighty Life," says Jakob Böhme.[8] "For when you strike upon the *sharp* part of the stone, the bitter sting of Nature sharpens itself, and is stirred in the highest degree. For Nature is dissipated or *broken asunder* in the sharpness, so that the *Liberty shines forth as a Flash.*" [9] The flash is the *"Birth of the light."* [10] It has transformative power: "For if I could in my Flesh comprehend the Flash, which I very well see and know how it is, I could clarify or transfigure my Body therewith, so that it would shine with a bright light and glory. And then it would no more resemble and be conformed to the bestial Body, but to the angels of God." [11] Elsewhere Böhme says: "As when the Flash of Life

4 Caesarius of Heisterbach, *The Dialogue on Miracles,* trans. by Scott and Bland, Dist. IV, c. xxxiv (p. 231) and Dist. I, c. xxxii (p. 42): "His soul was like a glassy spherical vessel, that had eyes before and behind." A collection of similar reports in Bozzano, *Popoli primitivi e Manifestazioni supernormali.*

5 Cf. my "Paracelsus as a Spiritual Phenomenon," par. 190 It is Hermes Kyllenios, who calls up the souls. The caduceus corresponds to the phallus. Cf. Hippolytus, *Elenchos,* V, 7, 30.

6 The same association in *Elenchos,* V, 16, 8: serpent = δύναμις of Moses.

7 Ruland (*Lexicon,* 1612) speaks of "the gliding of the mind or spirit into another world." In the *Chymical Wedding* of Rosencreutz the lightning causes the royal pair to come alive. The Messiah appears as lightning in the Syrian Apocalypse of Baruch (Charles, *Apocrypha,* II, p. 510). Hippolytus (*Elenchos,* VIII, 10, 3) says that, in the view of the Docetists, the Monogenes drew together "like the greatest lightning-flash into the smallest body" (because the Aeons could not stand the effulgence of the Pleroma), or like "light under the eyelids." In this form he came into the world through Mary (VIII, 10, 5). Lactantius (*Works,* trans. by Fletcher, I, p. 470) says: ". . . the light of the descending God may be manifest in all the world as lightning." This refers to Luke 17 : 24: ". . . as the lightning that lighteneth . . so shall the Son of man be in his day." Similarly Zach. 9 : 14: "And the Lord God . . . his dart shall go forth as lightning" (DV).

8 *Forty Questions concerning the Soul* (*Works,* ed. Ward and Langcake, II, p. 17).

9 *The High and Deep Searching of the Threefold Life of Man* (*Works,* II), p. 11.

10 *Aurora* (*Works,* I), X. 17, p. 84.   11 Ibid., X. 38, p. 86,

rises up in the centre of the Divine Power, wherein all the spirits of God attain their life, and highly rejoice." [12] Of the "Source-spirit" *Mercurius,* he says that it "arises in the Fire-flash." Mercurius is the "animal spirit" which, from *Lucifer's* body, "struck into the Salniter [13] of God like a *fiery serpent* from its hole, as if there went a fiery Thunder-bolt into God's Nature, or a fierce Serpent, which tyrannizes, raves, and rages, as if it would tear and rend Nature all to pieces." [14] Of the "innermost *birth of the soul*" the bestial body "attains only a glimpse, just as if it lightened." [15] "The triumphing *divine Birth* lasteth in us men only so long as the flash lasteth; therefore our knowledge is but in part, whereas in God the flash stands unchangeably, always eternally thus." [16] (Cf. Fig. 1.)

535   In this connection I would like to mention that Böhme associates lightning with something else too. That is the *quaternity,* which plays a great role in the following pictures. When caught and assuaged in the four "Qualities" or four "Spirits," [17] "the Flash, or the Light, subsists in the *Midst or Centre as a Heart.*[18] Now when that Light, which stands in the Midst or Centre, shines into the four Spirits, then the Power of the four Spirits rises up in the Light, and they become Living, and love the Light; that is, they take it into them, and are *impregnated* with it." [19] "The Flash, or *Stock,* [20] or Pith, or the Heart, which is generated in the Powers, remains standing in the Midst or Centre, and that is the *Son.* . . . And this is the true *Holy Ghost,* whom we Christians honour and adore for the third

---

[12] Ibid., X. 53, p. 87.

[13] Salniter = *sal nitri* = Saltpetre; like salt, *the prima materia. Three Principles of the Divine Essence (Works,* I), I. 9, p. 10.

[14] *Aurora,* XV. 84, p. 154. Here the lightning is not a revelation of God's will but a Satanic change of state. Lightning is also a manifestation of the devil (Luke 10 : 18).   [15] Ibid., XIX. 19, p. 185.   [16] Ibid., XI. 10, p. 93.

[17] For Böhme the four "qualities" coincide partly with the four elements but also with dry, wet, warm, cold, the four qualities of taste (e.g., sharp, bitter, sweet, sour), and the four colours.

[18] A heart forms the centre of the mandala in the *Forty Questions.* See Fig. 1.

[19] *Aurora,* XI. 27–28, p. 94.

[20] "Stock" in this context can mean tree or cross (σταυρός, 'stake, pole, post'), but it could also refer to a staff or stick. It would then be the magical wand that, in the subsequent development of these pictures, begins to sprout like a tree. Cf. infra, par. 570.

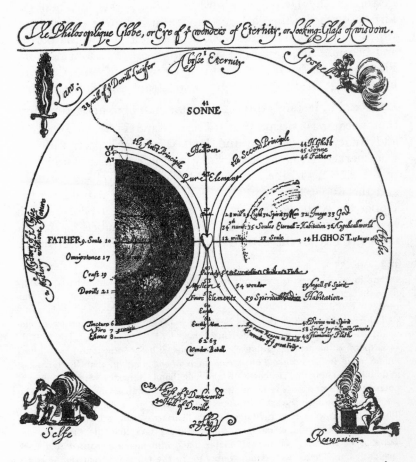

Fig. 1. Mandala from Jakob Böhme's *XL Questions concerning the Soule* (1620)

The picture is taken from the English edition of 1647. The quaternity consists of *Father, H. Ghost, Sonne,* and *Earth* or *Earthly Man.* It is characteristic that the two semicircles are turned back to back instead of closing.

Person in the Deity." [21] Elsewhere Böhme says: "When the Fire-flash reaches the dark substance,[22] it is a great terror, from which the Cold Fire draws back in affright as if it would perish, and becomes impotent, and sinks into itself. . . . But now the Flash . . . makes in its Rising a Cross [23] with the Comprehension of all Properties; for here arises the Spirit in the Essence, and it stands thus: ⊕. If thou hast here understanding, thou needest ask no more; it is Eternity and Time, God in Love and Anger, also Heaven and Hell. The lower part, which is thus marked ▽, is the first Principle, and is the Eternal Nature in the Anger, viz. the Kingdom of Darkness dwelling in itself; and the upper Part, with this figure ⚶, is the Salniter; [24] the Upper Cross above the Circle is the Kingdom of Glory, which in the Flagrat of Joy in the Will of the free Lubet [25] proceeds from the Fire in the Lustre of the Light into the power of the

---

[21] *Aurora*, XI. 37, p. 95.

[22] The lower darkness corresponds to the elemental world, which has a quaternary character. Cf. the four Achurayim mentioned in the commentary to Picture 7.

[23] The reason for this is that the lightning is caught by the quaternity of elements and qualities and so divided into four.

[24] Saltpetre is the arcane substance, synonymous with *Sal Saturni* and *Sal Tartari mundi maioris* (Khunrath, *Von hylealischen Chaos*, 1597, p. 263). Tartarus has a double meaning in alchemy: on the one hand it means tartar (hydrogen potassium tartrate); on the other, the lower half of the cooking vessel and also the arcane substance (Eleazar, *Uraltes Chymisches Werk*, 1760, II, p. 91, no. 32). The metals grow in the "cavitates terrae" (Tartarus). Salt, according to Khunrath, is the "centrum terrae physicum." Eleazar says that the "Heaven and Tartarus of the wise" change all metals back into mercury. Saturn is a dark "malefic" star. There is the same symbolism in the Offertory from the Mass for the Dead: "Deliver the souls of all the faithful departed from the pains of hell and from the deep pit; deliver them from the mouth of the lion [attribute of Ialdabaoth, Saturn], lest Tartarus lay hold on them, and they fall into darkness." Saturn "maketh darkness" (Böhme, *Threefold Life*, IX. 85, p. 96) and is one aspect of the Salniter (*Signatura rerum*, XIV. 46–48, p. 118). Salniter is the "dried" or "fixed" form and embodiment of the seven "Source Spirits" of God, who are all contained in the seventh, Mercury, the "Word of God" (*Aurora*, XI. 86f., p. 99 and XV. 49, p. 151; *Sig. rer.*, IV. 35, p. 28). Salniter, like mercury, is the mother and cause of all metals and salts (*Sig. rer.*, XIV. 46 and III. 16, pp. 118 and 19). It is a subtle body, the paradisal earth and the spotless state of the body before the Fall, and hence the epitome of the *prima materia*.

[25] ["Flagrat" and "lubet" are used by Böhme to signify respectively "flash, flame, burning" and "desire, affect."—EDITORS.]

Liberty; and this spiritual Water [26] . . . is the Corporality of the free Lubet . . . wherein the Lustre from the Fire and Light makes a Tincture, viz. a budding and growing and a Manifestation of Colours from the Fire and Light." [27]

536   I have purposely dwelt at some length on Böhme's disquisition on the lightning, because it throws a good deal of light on the psychology of our pictures. However, it anticipates some things that will only become clear when we examine the pictures themselves. I must therefore ask the reader to bear Böhme's views in mind in the following commentary. I have put the most important points in italics. It is clear from the quotations what the lightning meant to Böhme and what sort of a role it plays in the present case. The last quotation in particular deserves special attention, as it anticipates various key motifs in the subsequent pictures done by my patient, namely the cross, the quaternity, the divided mandala, the lower half of which is virtually equivalent to hell and the upper half to the lighter realm of the "Salniter." For Böhme the lower half signifies the "everlasting darkness" that "extends into the fire," [28] while the upper, "salnitrous" half corresponds to the third Principle, the "visible, elemental world, which is an emanation of the first and other Principle." [29] The cross, in turn, corresponds to the second Principle, the "Kingdom of Glory," which is revealed through "magic fire," the lightning, which he calls a "Revelation of Divine Motion." [30] The "lustre of the fire" comes from the "unity of God" and reveals his will. The mandala therefore represents the "Kingdom of Nature," which "in itself is the great everlasting Darkness." The "Kingdom of God," on the other hand, or the "Glory" (i.e., the Cross), is the Light of which John 1 : 5 speaks: "And the light shineth in the darkness, and the darkness comprehendeth it not." The Life that "breaks itself off from the eternal Light and enters into the Object, as into the selfhood of Properties," is "only fantastic and foolish, even such as the Devils were, and the souls of the damned are; as can be seen . . . from the fourth number." [31]

---

26 Reference to the "waters which were above the firmament" (Gen. 1 : 7).
27 Sig. rer., XIV. 32–33, p. 116.
28 Tabula principiorum, 3 (Amsterdam edn., 1682, p. 271).
29 Ibid., 5, p. 271.   30 Ibid., 42, p. 279.
31 Four Tables of Divine Revelation, p. 14.

For the "fire of Nature" is called by Böhme the *fourth form*, and he understands it as a "spiritual Life-Fire, that exists from a continual conjunction . . . of Hardness [i.e., the solidified, dry Salniter] and Motion [the Divine Will]." [32] Quite in keeping with John 1 : 5 the quaternity of the lightning, the Cross, pertains to the Kingdom of Glory, whereas Nature, the visible world and the dark abyss remain untouched by the fourfold light and abide in darkness.

537   For the sake of completeness I should mention that ☿ is the sign for *cinnabar*, the most important quicksilver ore (HgS).[33] The coincidence of the two symbols can hardly be accidental in view of the significance which Böhme attributes to Mercurius. Ruland finds it rather hard to define exactly what was meant by cinnabar.[34] The only certain thing is that there was a κιννάβαρις τῶν φιλοσόφων (cinnabar of the philosophers) in Greek alchemy, and that it stood for the *rubedo* stage of the transforming substance. Thus Zosimos says: "(After the preceding process) you will find the gold coloured fiery red like blood. That is the cinnabar of the philosophers and the copper man (χαλκάνθρωπος), turned to gold." [35] Cinnabar was also supposed to be identical with the uroboros dragon.[36] Even in Pliny, cinnabar is called *sanguis draconis*, 'dragon's blood,' a term that lasted all through the Middle Ages.[37] On account of its redness it was often identified with the philosophical sulphur. A special difficulty is the fact that the wine-red cinnabar crystals were classed with the ἄνθρακες, *carbons*, to which belong all reddish and red-tinted stones like *rubies*, garnets, amethysts, etc. They all shine like glowing coals.[38] The λιθάνθρακες (anthracites), on the other hand, were

---

32 Ibid., p. 13.

33 Its official name is *hydrargyrum sulfuratum rubrum*. Another version of its sign is ☿: cf. Lüdy, *Alchemistische und Chemische Zeichen*, and Gessmann, *Die Geheimsymbole der Alchymie, Arzneikunde und Astrologie des Mittelalters*.

34 "There is very great doubt among doctors as to what is actually signified by Cinnabar, for the term is applied by different authorities to very diverse substances." Ruland, *Lexicon*, p. 102.

35 Berthelot, *Alch. grecs*, III, xxix, 24.

36 Ibid., I, v, 1. It may be remarked that the dragon has three ears and four legs (The axiom of Maria! Cf. *Psychology and Alchemy*, pars. 209f.)

37 *Hist. nat.*, Lib. XXXIII, cap. vii.

38 The medical term *anthrax* means 'carbuncle, abscess.'

regarded as "quenched" coals. These associations explain the similarity of the alchemical signs for gold, antimony, and garnet. Gold ☉, after mercury the most important "philosophical" substance, shares its sign with what is known as "regulus" or "button" antimony,[39] and during the two decades prior to the writing of *Signatura rerum* (1622), from which our quotation comes, this had enjoyed particular fame as the new transformative substance[40] and panacea.[41] Basilius Valentinus' *Triumphal Car of Antimony* was published about the first decade of the seventeenth century (the first edition possibly in 1611) and soon found the widest acclaim.[42] The sign for garnet is ♁, and ⊖ means salt. A cross with a little circle in it ⊕ means copper (from the "Cyprian," Venus ♀). Medicinal tartaric acid is denoted by ♀, and hydrogen potassium tartrate (tartar) has the signs ⊖ ♃.[43] Tartar settles on the bottom of the vessel, which in the language of the alchemists means: in the underworld, Tartarus.[44]

538   I will not attempt here any interpretation of Böhme's symbols, but will only point out that in our picture the lightning, striking into the darkness and "hardness," has blasted a *rotundum* out of the dark *massa confusa* and kindled a light in it. There can be no doubt that the dark stone means the blackness, i.e., the unconscious, just as the sea and sky and the upper half of the woman's figure indicate the sphere of consciousness. We may safely assume that Böhme's symbol refers to a similar situation. The lightning has released the spherical form from the rock and so caused a kind of liberation. But, just as the magician has been replaced by the lightning, so the patient has been replaced by the sphere. The unconscious has thus presented her

---

[39] Antimony is also denoted by ♂. Regulus = "The impure mass of metal formed beneath the slag in melting and reducing ores" (Merriam-Webster).

[40] Michael Maier (*Symbola aureae mensae*, 1617, p. 380) says: "The true antimony of the Philosophers lies hidden in the deep sea, like the son of the King."

[41] Praised as Hercules Morbicida, "slayer of diseases" (ibid., p. 378).

[42] The book was (first?) mentioned by Maier, ibid., pp. 379ff.

[43] Also ⊡, a pure quaternity.

[44] Τάρταρος, like βόρβορος, βάρβαρος, etc. is probably onomatopoeic, expressing terror. Τάργανον means 'vinegar, spoilt wine.' Derived from ταράσσω, 'to stir up, disturb, frighten' (τάραγμα, 'trouble, confusion') and τάρβος, 'terror, awe.'

with ideas which show that she had gone on thinking without the aid of consciousness and that this radically altered the initial situation. It was again her inability to draw that led to this result. Before finding this solution, she had made two attempts to portray the act of liberation with human figures, but with no success. She had overlooked the fact that the initial situation, her imprisonment in the rock, was already irrational and symbolic and therefore could not be solved in a rational way. It had to be done by an equally irrational process. That was why I advised her, should she fail in her attempt to draw human figures, to use some kind of hieroglyph. It then suddenly struck her that the sphere was a suitable symbol for the individual human being. That it was a chance idea (*Einfall*) is proved by the fact that it was not her conscious mind that thought up this typification, but the unconscious, for an *Einfall* "falls in" quite of its own accord. It should be noted that she represents only herself as a sphere, not me. I am represented only by the lightning, purely functionally, so that for her I am simply the "precipitating" cause. As a magician I appeared to her in the apt role of Hermes Kyllenios, of whom the Odyssey says: "Meanwhile Cyllenian Hermes was gathering in the souls of the suitors, armed with the splendid golden wand that he can use at will to cast a spell on our eyes or wake us from the soundest sleep." [45] Hermes is the ψυχῶν αἴτιος, 'originator of souls.' He is also the ἡγήτωρ ὀνείρων, 'guide of dreams.' [46] For the following pictures it is of special importance that Hermes has the number 4 attributed to him. Martianus Capella says: "The number four is assigned to the Cyllenian, for he alone is held to be a fourfold god." [47]

539   The form the picture had taken was not unreservedly welcome to the patient's conscious mind. Luckily, however, while painting it Miss X had discovered that two factors were involved. These, in her own words, were *reason* and the *eyes*. Reason always wanted to make the picture as *it* thought it ought to be; but the eyes held fast to their vision and finally forced the picture to come out as it actually did and not in accordance with rationalistic expectations. Her reason, she said, had really intended a daylight scene, with the sunshine melting the sphere

[45] Rieu trans., p. 351.
[46] Hippolytus, *Elenchos*, V, 7, 30; Kerényi, "Hermes der Seelenführer," p. 29.
[47] Ibid., p. 30.

free, but the eyes favoured a nocturne with "shattering, dangerous lightning." This realization helped her to acknowledge the actual result of her artistic efforts and to admit that it was in fact an objective and impersonal process and not a personal relationship.

540 For anyone with a personalistic view of psychic events, such as a Freudian, it will not be easy to see in this anything more than an elaborate repression. But if there was any repression here we certainly cannot make the conscious mind responsible for it, because the conscious mind would undoubtedly have preferred a personal imbroglio as being far more interesting. The repression must have been manoeuvred by the unconscious from the start. One should consider what this means: instinct, the most original force of the unconscious, is suppressed or turned back on itself by an arrangement stemming from this same unconscious! It would be idle indeed to talk of "repression" here, since we know that the unconscious goes straight for its goal and that this does not consist solely in pairing two animals but in allowing an individual to become whole. For this purpose wholeness—represented by the sphere—is emphasized as the essence of personality, while I am reduced to the fraction of a second, the duration of a lightning flash.

541 The patient's association to lightning was that it might stand for *intuition,* a conjecture that is not far off the mark, since intuitions often come "like a flash." Moreover, there are good grounds for thinking that Miss X was a *sensation* type. She herself thought she was one. The "inferior" function would then be intuition. As such, it would have the significance of a releasing or "redeeming" function. We know from experience that the inferior function always compensates, complements, and balances the "superior" function.[48] My psychic peculiarity would make me a suitable projection carrier in this respect. The inferior function is the one of which least conscious use is made. This is the reason for its undifferentiated quality, but also for its freshness and vitality. It is not at the disposal of the conscious mind, and even after long use it never loses its autonomy and spontaneity, or only to a very limited degree. Its role is therefore mostly that of a *deus ex machina.* It depends not on the

48 The pairs of functions are thinking/feeling, sensation/intuition. See *Psychological Types,* definitions.

ego but on the *self*. Hence it hits consciousness unexpectedly, like lightning, and occasionally with devastating consequences. It thrusts the ego aside and makes room for a supraordinate factor, the totality of a person, which consists of conscious and unconscious and consequently extends far beyond the ego. This self was always present,[49] but sleeping, like Nietzsche's "image in the stone." [50] It is, in fact, the secret of the stone, of the *lapis philosophorum*, in so far as this is the *prima materia*. In the stone sleeps the spirit *Mercurius*, the "circle of the moon," the "round and square," [51] the homunculus, Tom Thumb and Anthropos at once,[52] whom the alchemists also symbolized as their famed *lapis philosophorum*.[53]

542   All these ideas and inferences were naturally unknown to my patient, and they were known to me at the time only in so far as I was able to recognize the circle as a *mandala*,[54] the psychological expression of the totality of the self. Under these circumstances there could be no question of my having unintentionally infected her with alchemical ideas. The pictures are, in all essentials, genuine creations of the unconscious; their inessential aspects (landscape motifs) are derived from conscious contents.

543   Although the sphere with its glowing red centre and the golden flash of lightning play the chief part, it should not be overlooked that there are several other eggs or spheres as well. If the sphere signifies the self of the patient, we must apply this interpretation to the other spheres, too. They must therefore represent other people who, in all probability, were her intimates. In both the pictures two other spheres are clearly indicated. So I must mention that Miss X had two women friends who shared her intellectual interests and were joined to her in a lifelong friendship. All three of them, as if bound together by fate, are rooted in the same "earth," i.e., in the collective unconscious, which is one and the same for all. It is probably for this reason that the second picture has the decidedly *nocturnal*

---

[49] Cf. *Psychology and Alchemy*, par. 329, for the *a priori* presence of the mandala symbol.   [50] Details in ibid., par. 406.

[51] Preisendanz, *Papyri Graecae Magicae*, II, p. 139.

[52] "The Spirit Mercurius," pars. 267ff.

[53] *Psychology and Alchemy*, Part III, ch. 5.

[54] Cf. Wilhelm and Jung, *The Secret of the Golden Flower*.

character intended by the unconscious and asserted against the wishes of the conscious mind. It should also be mentioned that the pointed pyramids of the first picture reappear in the second, where their points are actually gilded by the lightning and strongly emphasized. I would interpret them as unconscious contents "pushing up" into the light of consciousness, as seems to be the case with many contents of the collective unconscious.[55] In contrast to the first picture, the second is painted in more vivid colours, red and gold. Gold expresses sunlight, value, divinity even. It is therefore a favourite synonym for the *lapis*, being the *aurum philosophicum* or *aurum potabile* or *aurum vitreum*.[56]

544   As already pointed out, I was not at that time in a position to reveal anything of these ideas to Miss X, for the simple reason that I myself knew nothing of them. I feel compelled to mention this circumstance yet again, because the third picture, which now follows, brings a motif that points unmistakably to alchemy and actually gave me the definitive incentive to make a thorough study of the works of the old adepts.

Picture 3

545   The third picture, done as spontaneously as the first two, is distinguished most of all by its light colours. Free-floating in space, among clouds, is a dark blue sphere with a wine-red border. Round the middle runs a wavy silver band, which keeps the sphere balanced by "equal and opposite forces," as the patient explained. To the right, above the sphere, floats a snake with golden rings, its head pointing at the sphere—an obvious development of the golden lightning in Picture 2. But she drew the snake in afterwards, on account of certain "reflections." The whole is "a planet in the making." In the middle of the silver band is the number 12. The band was thought of as being in rapid vibratory motion; hence the wave motif. It is like a vibrating belt that keeps the sphere afloat. Miss X compared it to the ring of Saturn. But unlike this, which is composed of

---

[55] Though we talk a great deal and with some justice about the resistance which the unconscious puts up against becoming conscious, it must also be emphasized that it has a kind of gradient towards consciousness, and this acts as an urge to become conscious.

[56] The last-named refers to Rev. 21 : 21.

disintegrated satellites, her ring was the origin of future moons such as Jupiter possesses. The black lines in the silver band she called "lines of force"; they were meant to indicate that it was in motion. As if asking a question, I made the remark: "Then it is the vibrations of the band that keep the sphere floating?" "Naturally," she said, "they are the wings of Mercury, the messenger of the gods. The silver is *quicksilver!*" She went on at once: "Mercury, that is Hermes, is the Nous, the mind or reason, and that is the animus, who is here outside instead of inside. He is like a veil that hides the true personality." [57] We shall leave this latter remark alone for the moment and turn first to the wider context, which, unlike that of the two previous pictures, is especially rich.

546   While Miss X was painting this picture, she felt that two earlier dreams were mingling with her vision. They were the two "big" dreams of her life. She knew of the attribute "big" from my stories of the dream life of African primitives I had visited. It has become a kind of "colloquial term" for characterizing archetypal dreams, which as we know have a peculiar numinosity. It was used in this sense by the dreamer. Several years previously, she had undergone a major operation. Under narcosis she had the following dream-vision: *She saw a grey globe of the world. A silver band rotated about the equator and, according to the frequency of its vibrations, formed alternate zones of condensation and evaporation. In the zones of condensation appeared the numbers 1 to 3, but they had the tendency to increase up to 12.* These numbers signified "nodal points" or "great personalities" who played a part in man's historical development. "The number 12 meant the most important nodal point or great man (still to come), because it denotes the climax or turning point of the process of development." (These are her own words.)

547   The other dream that intervened had occurred a year before the first one: *She saw a golden snake in the sky. It demanded the sacrifice, from among a great crowd of people, of a young man, who obeyed this demand with an expression of sorrow.* The dream was repeated a little later, but this time *the snake*

---

[57] Miss X was referring to my remarks in "The Relations between the Ego and the Unconscious," which she knew in its earlier version in *Collected Papers on Analytical Psychology* (2nd. edn., 1920).

Picture 1

Picture 2

Picture 3

Picture 4

Picture 5

Picture 6

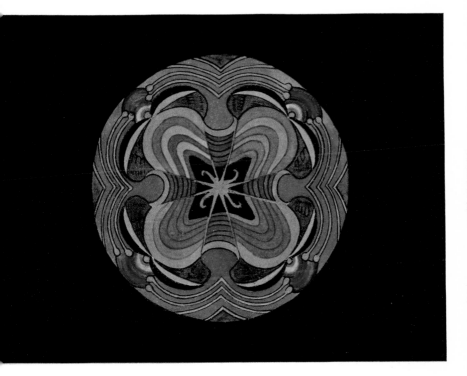

Picture 7

Picture 8

Picture 9

Picture 10

Picture 11

Picture 12

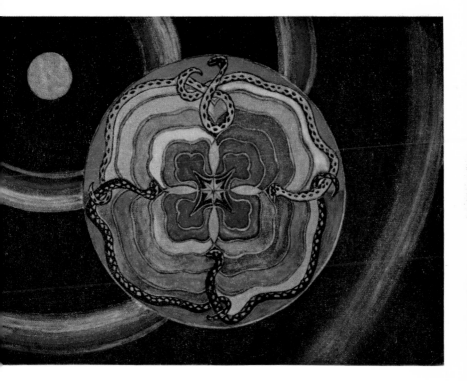

Picture 13

Picture 14

Picture 15

Picture 16

Picture 17

Picture 18

Picture 19

Picture 20

Picture 21

Picture 22

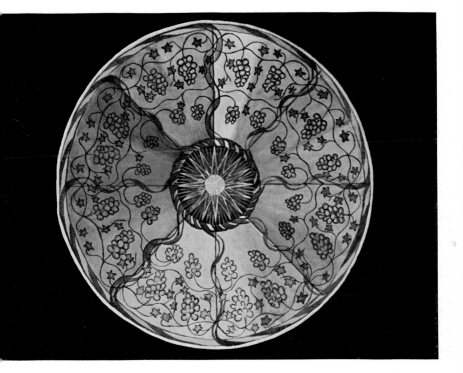

Picture 23

Picture 24

picked on the dreamer herself. The assembled people regarded her compassionately, but she took her fate "proudly" on herself.

548   She was, as she told me, born immediately after midnight, so soon afterwards, indeed, that there was some doubt as to whether she came into the world on the 28th or on the 29th. Her father used to tease her by saying that she was obviously born before her time, since she came into the world just at the beginning of a new day, but "only just," so that one could almost believe she was born "at the twelfth hour." The number 12, as she said, meant for her the culminating point of her life, which she had only now reached. That is, she felt the "liberation" as the climax of her life. It is indeed an hour of birth—not of the dreamer but of the self. This distinction must be borne in mind.

549   The context to Picture 3 here established needs a little commentary. First, it must be emphasized that the patient felt the moment of painting this picture as the "climax" of her life and also described it as such. Second, two "big" dreams have amalgamated in the picture, which heightens its significance still more. The sphere blasted from the rock in Picture 2 has now, in the brighter atmosphere, floated up to heaven. The nocturnal darkness of the earth has vanished. The increase of light indicates conscious realization: the liberation has become a fact that is integrated into consciousness. The patient has understood that the floating sphere symbolizes the "true personality." At present, however, it is not quite clear how she understands the relation of the ego to the "true personality." The term chosen by her coincides in a remarkable way with the Chinese *chen-yen*, the "true" or "complete" man, who has the closest affinity with the *homo quadratus* [58] of alchemy.[59] As we pointed out in the analysis of Picture 2, the *rotundum* of alchemy is identical with Mercurius, the "round and square." [60] In Picture 3 the connection is shown concretely through the

58 The expressions "square," "four-square," are used in English in this sense.
59 The "squared figure" in the centre of the alchemical mandala, symbolizing the *lapis,* and whose midpoint is Mercurius, is called the "mediator making peace between the enemies or elements." [Cf. *Aion* (Part II of vol. 9), pars. 377f.— EDITORS.]
60 So called in an invocation to Hermes. Cf. Preisendanz, II, p. 139. Further particulars in *Psychology and Alchemy,* par. 172; fig. 214 is a repetition of the *quadrangulum secretum sapientum* from the *Tractatus aureus* (1610), p. 43. Cf. also my "The Spirit Mercurius," par. 272.

mediating idea of the wings of Mercury, who, it is evident, has entered the picture in his own right and not because of any non-existent knowledge of Böhme's writings.[61]

550   For the alchemists the process of individuation represented by the *opus* was an analogy of the creation of the world, and the *opus* itself an analogy of God's work of creation. Man was seen as a microcosm, a complete equivalent of the world in miniature. In our picture, we see what it is in man that corresponds to the cosmos, and what kind of evolutionary process is compared with the creation of the world and the heavenly bodies: it is the *birth of the self,* the latter appearing as a microcosm.[62] It is not the empirical man that forms the "correspondentia" to the world, as the medievalists thought, but rather the indescribable totality of the psychic or spiritual man, who cannot be described because he is compounded of consciousness as well as of the indeterminable extent of the unconscious.[63] The term microcosm proves the existence of a common intuition (also present in my patient) that the "total" man is as big as the world, like an Anthropos. The cosmic analogy had already appeared in the much earlier dream under narcosis, which likewise contained the problem of personality: the nodes of the vibrations were great personalities of historical importance. As early as 1916, I had observed a similar individuation process, illustrated by pictures, in another woman patient. In her case too there was a world creation, depicted as follows (see Fig. 2):

551   To the left, from an unknown source, three drops fall, dissolving into four lines,[64] or two pairs of lines. These lines move and form four separate paths, which then unite periodically in a nodal point and thus build a system of vibrations. The nodes are "great personalities and founders of religions," as my erstwhile patient told me. It is obviously the same conception as in our case, and we can call it archetypal in so far as there exist

[61] Despite my efforts I could find no other source for the "mercury." Naturally cryptomnesia cannot be ruled out. Considering the definiteness of the idea and the astonishing coincidence of its appearance (as in Böhme), I incline to the hypothesis of spontaneous emergence, which does not eliminate the archetype but, on the contrary, presupposes it.

[62] Cf. the "innermost Birth of the Soul" in Böhme.

[63] This *homo interior* or *altus* was Mercurius, or was at least derived from him. Cf. "The Spirit Mercurius," pars. 284ff.

[64] The lines are painted in the classical four colours.

Fig. 2. Sketch of a picture from the year 1916

At the top, the sun, surrounded by a rainbow-coloured halo divided into twelve parts, like the zodiac. To the left, the descending, to the right, the ascending, transformation process.

universal ideas of world periods, critical transitions, gods and half gods who personify the aeons. The unconscious naturally does not produce its images from conscious reflections, but from the worldwide propensity of the human system to form such conceptions as the world periods of the Parsees, the yugas and avatars of Hinduism, and the Platonic months of astrology with their bull and ram deities and the "great" Fish of the Christian aeon.[65]

552   That the nodes in our patient's picture signify or contain numbers is a bit of unconscious number mysticism that is not always easy to unravel. So far as I can see, there are two stages in this arithmetical phenomenology: the first, earlier stage goes up to 3, the second, later stage up to 12. Two numbers, 3 and 12, are expressly mentioned. Twelve is four times three. I think we have here stumbled again on the axiom of Maria, that peculiar dilemma of three and four,[66] which I have discussed many times before because it plays such a great role in alchemy.[67] I would hazard that we have to do here with a *tetrameria* (as in Greek alchemy), a transformation process divided into four stages [68] of three parts each, analogous to the twelve transformations of the zodiac and its division into four. As not infrequently happens, the number 12 would then have a not merely individual significance (as the patient's birth number, for instance), but a time-conditioned one too, since the present aeon of the Fishes is drawing to its end and is at the same time the twelfth house of the zodiac. One is reminded of similar Gnostic ideas, such as those in the gnosis of Justin: The "Father" (Elohim) begets with Edem, who was half woman and half snake, twelve "fatherly" angels, and Edem gives birth besides these to twelve "motherly" angels, who—in psychological parlance—represent the shadows of the twelve "fatherly" ones. The "motherly" angels divide themselves into four categories (μέρη) of three each, corresponding to the four rivers of

65 The "giant" fish of the Abercius inscription (*c.* A.D. 200). [Cf. *Aion*, par. 127, n. 4.—EDITORS.]
66 Cf. Frobenius, *Schicksalskunde*, pp. 119f. The author's interpretations seem to me questionable in some respects.
67 *Psychology and Alchemy*, par. 204; "The Phenomenology of the Spirit in Fairytales," pars. 425 and 430; and *Psychology and Religion*, par. 184.
68 *Psychology and Alchemy*, index, s.v. "quartering."

Paradise. These angels dance round in a circle (ἐν χόρῳ κυκλικῷ).[69] It is legitimate to bring these seemingly remote associations into hypothetical relationship, because they all spring from a common root, i.e., the collective unconscious.

553 In our picture Mercurius forms a world-encircling band, usually represented by a snake.[70] Mercurius is a serpent or dragon in alchemy ("serpens mercurialis"). Oddly enough, this serpent is some distance away from the sphere and is aiming down at it, as if to strike. The sphere, we are told, is kept afloat by equal and opposite forces, represented by the quicksilver or somehow connected with it. According to the old view, Mercurius is duplex, i.e., he is himself an antithesis.[71] Mercurius or Hermes is a magician and god of magicians. As Hermes Trismegistus he is the patriarch of alchemy. His magician's wand, the caduceus, is entwined by two snakes. The same attribute distinguishes Asklepios, the god of physicians.[72] The archetype of these ideas was projected on to me by the patient before ever the analysis had begun.

554 The primordial image underlying the sphere girdled with quicksilver is probably that of the world egg encoiled by a snake.[73] But in our case the snake symbol of Mercurius is replaced by a sort of pseudo-physicistic notion of a field of vibrating molecules of quicksilver. This looks like an intellectual disguising of the true situation, that the self, or its symbol, is

[69] Hippolytus, *Elenchos*, V, 26, 1ff.

[70] Cf. the "account . . . of a many-coloured and many-shaped sphere" from the Cod. Vat. 190 (cited by Cumont in *Textes et monuments figurés relatifs aux mystères de Mithra*), which says: "The all-wise God fashioned an immensely great dragon of gigantic length, breadth and thickness, having its dark-coloured head . . . towards sunrise, and its tail . . . towards sunset." Of the dragon the text says: "Then the all-wise Demiurge, by his highest command, set in motion the great dragon with the spangled crown, I mean the twelve signs of the zodiac which it carried on its back." Eisler (*Weltenmantel und Himmelszelt*, p. 389) connects this zodiacal serpent with Leviathan. For the dragon as symbol of the year, see the Mythographus Vaticanus III, in *Classicorum Auctorum e Vaticanis Codicibus Editorum*, VI (1831), p. 162. There is a similar association in Horapollo, *Hieroglyphica*, trans. by Boas, p. 57.   [71] "The Spirit Mercurius," ch. 6.

[72] Meier, *Ancient Incubation and Modern Psychotherapy*.

[73] Vishnu is described as *dāmodara*, 'bound about the body with a rope.' I am not sure whether this symbol should be considered here; I mention it only for the sake of completeness.

entwined by the mercurial serpent. As the patient remarked more or less correctly, the "true personality" is veiled by it. This, presumably, would then be something like an Eve in the coils of the paradisal serpent. In order to avoid giving this appearance, Mercurius has obligingly split into his two forms, according to the old-established pattern: the *mercurius crudus* or *vulgi* (crude or ordinary quicksilver), and the *Mercurius Philosophorum* (the *spiritus mercurialis* or the spirit Mercurius, Hermes-Nous), who hovers in the sky as the golden lightning-snake or Nous Serpent, at present inactive. In the vibrations of the quicksilver band we may discern a certain tremulous excitement, just as the suspension expresses tense expectation: "Hover and haver suspended in pain!" For the alchemists quicksilver meant the concrete, material manifestation of the spirit Mercurius, as the above-mentioned mandala in the scholia to the *Tractatus aureus* shows: the central point is Mercurius, and the square is Mercurius divided into the four elements. He is the *anima mundi,* the innermost point and at the same time the encompasser of the world, like the atman in the Upanishads. And just as quicksilver is a materialization of Mercurius, so the gold is a materialization of the sun in the earth.[74]

555   A circumstance that never ceases to astonish one is this: that at all times and in all places alchemy brought its conception of the *lapis* or its *minera* (raw material) together with the idea of the *homo altus* or *maximus,* that is, with the Anthropos.[75] Equally, one must stand amazed at the fact that here too the conception of the dark round stone blasted out of the rock should represent such an abstract idea as the psychic totality of man. The earth and in particular the heavy cold stone is the epitome of materiality, and so is the metallic quicksilver which, the patient thought, meant the animus (mind, *nous*). We would expect pneumatic symbols for the idea of the self and the animus, images of air, breath, wind. The ancient formula λίθος οὐ λίθος (the stone that is no stone) expresses this dilemma: we are dealing with a *complexio oppositorum,* with something like the nature of light, which under some conditions behaves like particles and under others like waves, and is obviously in

[74] Michael Maier, *De circulo physico quadrato* (1616), ch. I.
[75] Christ in medieval alchemy. Cf. *Psychology and Alchemy,* Part III, ch. 5.

its essence both at once. Something of this kind must be conjectured with regard to these paradoxical and hardly explicable statements of the unconscious. They are not inventions of any conscious mind, but are spontaneous manifestations of a psyche not controlled by consciousness and obviously possessing all the freedom it wants to express views that take no account of our conscious intentions. The duplicity of Mercurius, his simultaneously metallic and pneumatic nature, is a parallel to the symbolization of an extremely spiritual idea like the Anthropos by a corporeal, indeed metallic, substance (gold). One can only conclude that the unconscious tends to regard spirit and matter not merely as equivalent but as actually identical, and this in flagrant contrast to the intellectual one-sidedness of consciousness, which would sometimes like to spiritualize matter and at other times to materialize spirit. That the *lapis,* or in our case the floating sphere, has a double meaning is clear from the circumstance that it is characterized by two symbolical colours: red means blood and affectivity, the physiological reaction that joins spirit to body, and blue means the spiritual process (mind or *nous*). This duality reminds one of the alchemical duality *corpus* and *spiritus,* joined together by a third, the *anima* as the *ligamentum corporis et spiritus.* For Böhme a "high deep blue" mixed with green signifies "Liberty," that is, the inner "Kingdom of Glory" of the reborn soul. Red leads to the region of fire and the "abyss of darkness," which forms the periphery of Böhme's mandala (see Fig. 1).

Picture 4

556   Picture 4, which now follows, shows a significant change: the sphere has divided into an outer membrane and an inner nucleus. The outer membrane is flesh coloured, and the originally rather nebulous red nucleus in Picture 2 now has a differentiated internal structure of a decidedly ternary character. The "lines of force" that originally belonged to the band of quicksilver now run through the whole nuclear body, indicating that the excitation is no longer external only but has seized the innermost core. "An enormous inner activity now began," the patient told me. The nucleus with its ternary structure is presumably the female organ, stylized to look like a plant, in the act of fecundation: the spermatozoon is penetrating the

29

nuclear membrane. Its role is played by the mercurial serpent: the snake is black, dark, chthonic, a subterranean and ithyphallic Hermes; but it has the golden wings of Mercury and consequently possesses his pneumatic nature. The alchemists accordingly represented their *Mercurius duplex* as the winged and wingless dragon, calling the former feminine and the latter masculine.

557   The serpent in our picture represents not so much the spermatozoon but, more accurately, the phallus. Leone Ebreo,[76] in his *Dialoghi d'amore*, calls the planet Mercury the *membrum virile* of heaven, that is, of the macrocosm conceived as the *homo maximus*.[77] The spermatozoon seems, rather, to correspond to the golden substance which the snake is injecting into the invaginated ectoderm of the nucleus.[78] The two silver petals (?) probably represent the receptive vessel, the moon-bowl in which the sun's seed (gold) is destined to rest.[79] Underneath the flower is a small violet circle inside the ovary, indicating by its colour that it is a "united double nature," spirit and body (blue and red).[80] The snake has a pale yellow halo, which is meant to express its numinosity.

558   Since the snake evolved out of the flash of lightning or is a modulated form of it, I would like to instance a parallel where the lightning has the same illuminating, vivifying, fertilizing, transforming and healing function that in our case falls to the snake (cf. Fig. 3). Two phases are represented: first, a black sphere, signifying a state of profound depression; and second, the lightning that strikes into this sphere. Ordinary speech

[76] The writings of the physician and philosopher Leone Ebreo (*c.* 1460–1520) enjoyed widespread popularity in the sixteenth century and exercised a far-reaching influence on his contemporaries and their successors. His work is a continuation of the Neoplatonist thought developed by the physician and alchemist Marsilio Ficino (1433–99) in his commentary on Plato's *Symposium*. Ebreo's real name was Don Judah Abrabanel, of Lisbon. (Sometimes the texts have Abrabanel, sometimes Abarbanel.)

[77] Cf. the English version, *The Philosophy of Love*, trans. by Friedeberg-Seeley and Barnes, pp. 92 and 94. The source of this view can be found in the cabalistic interpretation of Yesod (Knorr von Rosenroth, *Kabbala Denudata*, 1677–84).

[78] This pseudo-biological terminology fits in with the patient's scientific education.

[79] Another alchemical idea: the *synodos Lunae cum Sole*, or hierogamy of sun and moon. Cf. "The Psychology of the Transference," par. 421, n. 17.

[80] More on this in "On the Nature of the Psyche," par. 498.

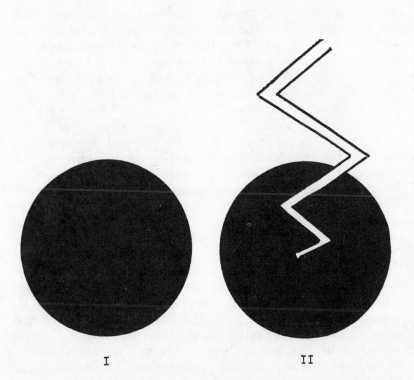

I   II

Fig. 3. Sketch of a drawing by a young woman patient with psychogenic depression from the beginning of the treatment

I. State of black hopelessness / II. Beginning of the therapeutic effect

In an earlier picture the sphere lay on the bottom of the sea. As a series of pictures shows, it arose in the first place because a black snake had swallowed the sun. There then followed an eight-rayed, completely black mandala with a wreath of eight silver stars. In the centre was a black homunculus. Next the black sphere developed a red centre, from which red rays, or streams of blood, ran out into tentacle-like extremities. The whole thing looked rather like a crab or an octopus. As the later pictures showed, the patient herself was shut up in the sphere.

makes use of the same imagery: something "strikes home" in a "flash of revelation." The only difference is that generally the image comes first, and only afterwards the realization which enables the patient to say: "This has struck home."

559   As to the context of Picture 4, Miss X emphasized that what disturbed her most was the band of quicksilver in Picture 3. She felt the silvery substance ought to be "inside," the black lines of force remaining outside to form a black snake. This would now encircle the sphere.[81] She felt the snake at first as a "terrible danger," as something threatening the "integrity of the sphere." At the point where the snake penetrates the nuclear membrane, fire breaks out (emotion). Her conscious mind interpreted this conflagration as a defensive reaction on the part of the sphere, and accordingly she tried to depict the attack as having been repulsed. But this attempt failed to satisfy the "eyes," though she showed me a pencil sketch of it. She was obviously in a dilemma: she could not accept the snake, because its sexual significance was only too clear to her without any assistance from me. I merely remarked to her: "This is a well-known process [82] which you can safely accept," and showed her from my collection a similar picture, done by a man, of a floating sphere being penetrated *from below* by a black phallus-like object. Later she said: "I suddenly understood the whole process in a more impersonal way." It was the realization of a law of life to which sex is subordinated. "The ego was not the centre, but, following a universal law, I circled round a sun." Thereupon she was able to accept the snake "as a necessary part of the process of growth" and finish the picture quickly and satisfactorily. Only one thing continued to give difficulty: she had to put the snake, she said, "One hundred per cent at the top, in the middle, in order to satisfy the eyes." Evidently the unconscious would only be satisfied with the most important position at the top and in the middle—in direct contrast to the picture

[81] Here one must think of the world-encircling Ocean and the world-snake hidden in it: Leviathan, the "dragon in the sea," which, in accordance with the Egyptian tradition of Typhon (Set) and the sea he rules over, is the devil. "The devil . . . surrounds the seas and the ocean on all sides" (St. Jerome, *Epistolae*, Part I, p. 12). Further particulars in Rahner, "Antenna Crucis II: Das Meer der Welt," pp. 89ff.

[82] We find the same motif in the two mandalas published by Esther Harding in *Psychic Energy: Its Source and Its Transformation* [Pls. XVI, XVII].

I had previously shown her. This, as I said, was done by a man and showed the menacing black symbol entering the mandala from below. For a woman, the typical danger emanating from the unconscious comes *from above*, from the "spiritual" sphere personified by the animus, whereas for a man it comes from the chthonic realm of the "world and woman," i.e., the anima projected on to the world.

560 Once again we must recall similar ideas found in Justin's gnosis: the third of the fatherly angels is Baruch. He is also the tree of life in paradise. His counterpart on the motherly side is Naas, the serpent, who is the tree of knowledge of good and evil.[83] When Elohim left Edem, because, as the second member, he had retreated to the first member of the divine triad (which consisted of the "Good," the "Father," and Edem), Edem pursued the pneuma of the Father, which he had left behind in man, and caused it to be tormented by Naas (ἵνα πάσαις κολάσεσι κολάζῃ τὸ ὂν πνεῦμα τοῦ Ἐλωεὶμ τὸ ἐν τοῖς ἀνθρώποις). Naas defiled Eve and also used Adam as a catamite. Edem, however, is the soul; Elohim is spirit. "The soul is against the spirit, and the spirit against the soul" (κατὰ τῆς ψυχῆς τετάκται).[84] This idea sheds light on the polarity of red and blue in our mandala, and also on the attack by the snake, who represents knowledge. That is why we fear knowledge of the truth, in this case, of the shadow. Therefore Baruch sent to mankind Jesus, that they might be led back to the "Good." But the "Good One is Priapus."[85] Elohim is the swan, Edem is Leda; he the gold, she Danae. Nor should we forget that the god of revelation has from of old the form of a snake—e.g., the *agathodaimon*. Edem too, as a snake-maiden, has a dual nature, "two-minded, two-bodied" (δίγνωμος, δίσωμος), and in medieval alchemy her figure became the symbol of the androgynous Mercurius.[86]

561 Let us remember that in Picture 3 *Mercurius vulgi*, ordinary quicksilver, encircles the sphere. This means that the mysterious

---

83 Naas is the same as the snakelike Nous and mercurial serpent of alchemy.
84 Hippolytus, *Elenchos*, V, 26, 21ff. This tale of Adam and Eve and the serpent was preserved until well into the Middle Ages.
85 Apparently a play on the words Πρίαπος and ἐπριοποίησε τὰ πάντα ('created all'). *Elenchos*, V, 26, 33.
86 See the illustration from Reusner's *Pandora* (1588) in my "Paracelsus as a Spiritual Phenomenon," Fig. B4.

sphere is enveloped or veiled by a "vulgar" or crude understanding. The patient herself opined that "the animus veils the true personality." We shall hardly be wrong in assuming that a banal, everyday view of the world, allegedly biological, has here got hold of the sexual symbol and concretized it after the approved pattern. A pardonable error! Another, more correct view is so much more subtle that one naturally prefers to fall back on something well-known and ready to hand, thus gratifying one's own "rational" expectations and earning the applause of one's contemporaries—only to discover that one has got hopelessly stuck and has arrived back at the point from which one set forth on the great adventure. It is clear what is meant by the ithyphallic serpent: from above comes all that is aerial, intellectual, spiritual, and from below all that is passionate, corporeal, and dark. The snake, contrary to expectation, turns out to be a pneumatic symbol,[87] a *Mercurius spiritualis*—a realization which the patient herself formulated by saying that the ego, despite its capricious manipulation of sexuality, is subject to a universal law. Sex in this case is therefore no problem at all, as it has been subjected to a higher transformation process and is contained in it; not repressed, only without an object.

562   Miss X subsequently told me that she felt Picture 4 was the most difficult, as if it denoted the turning point of the whole process. In my view she may not have been wrong in this, because the clearly felt, ruthless setting aside of the so beloved and so important ego is no light matter. Not for nothing is this "letting go" the *sine qua non* of all forms of higher spiritual development, whether we call it meditation, contemplation, yoga, or spiritual exercises. But, as this case shows, relinquishing the ego is not an act of the will and not a result arbitrarily produced; it is an event, an occurrence, whose inner, compelling logic can be disguised only by wilful self-deception.

563   In this case and at this moment the ability to "let go" is of decisive importance. But since everything passes, the moment may come when the relinquished ego must be reinstated in its functions. Letting go gives the unconscious the opportunity it

---

[87] In accordance with the classical view that the snake is πνευματικώτατον ζῷον, 'the most spiritual animal.' For this reason it was a symbol for the Nous and the Redeemer.

34

has been waiting for. But since it consists of opposites—day and night, bright and dark, positive and negative—and is good and evil and therefore ambivalent, the moment will infallibly come when the individual, like the exemplary Job, must hold fast so as not to be thrown catastrophically off balance—when the wave rebounds. The holding fast can be achieved only by a conscious will, i.e., by the ego. That is the great and irreplaceable significance of the ego, but one which, as we see here, is nonetheless relative. Relative, too, is the gain won by integrating the unconscious. We add to ourselves a bright and a dark, and more light means more night.[88] The urge of consciousness towards wider horizons, however, cannot be stopped; they must needs extend the scope of the personality, if they are not to shatter it.

Picture 5

564   Picture 5, Miss X said, followed naturally from Picture 4, with no difficulty. The sphere and the snake have drawn apart. The snake is sinking downwards and seems to have lost its threateningness. But the sphere has been fecundated with a vengeance: it has not only got bigger, but blossoms in the most vivid colours.[89] The nucleus has divided into four; something like a segmentation has occurred. This is not due to any conscious reflection, such as might come naturally to a biologically educated person; the division of the process or of the central symbol into four has always existed, beginning with the four sons of Horus, or the four seraphim of Ezekiel, or the birth of the four Aeons from the Metra (uterus) impregnated by the pneuma in Barbelo-Gnosis, or the cross formed by the lightning (snake) in Böhme's system,[90] and ending with the tetrameria of the *opus alchymicum* and its components (the four elements, qualities, stages, etc.).[91] In each case the quaternity forms a

88 Cf. what St. John of the Cross says about the "dark night of the soul." His interpretation is as helpful as it is psychological.

89 Hence the alchemical mandala was likened to a *rosarium* (rose-garden).

90 In Buddhism the "four great kings" (*lokapata*), the world-guardians, form the quaternity. Cf. the *Samyutta-Nikaya*, in *Dialogues of the Buddha*, Part II, p. 242.

91 "God separated and divided this primordial water by a kind of mystical distillation into four parts and regions" (Sendivogius, *Epist. XIII*, in Manget, *Bibliotheca chemica*, 1702, II, p. 496). In Christianos (Berthelot, *Alch. grecs*, VI, ix, 1 and x, 1) the egg, and matter itself, consist of four components. (Cited from Xenocrates, ibid., VI, xv, 8.)

unity; here it is the green circle at the centre of the four. The four are undifferentiated, and each of them forms a vortex, apparently turning to the left. I think I am not mistaken in regarding it as probable that, in general, a leftward movement indicates movement towards the unconscious, while a rightward (clockwise) movement goes towards consciousness.[92] The one is "sinister," the other "right," "rightful," "correct." In Tibet, the leftward-moving swastika is a sign of the Bön religion, of black magic. Stupas and chörtens must therefore be circumambulated clockwise. The leftward-spinning eddies spin into the unconscious; the rightward-spinning ones spin out of the unconscious chaos. The rightward-moving swastika in Tibet is therefore a Buddhist emblem.[93] (Cf. also Fig. 4.)

565   For our patient the process appeared to mean, first and foremost, a differentiation of consciousness. From the treasures of her psychological knowledge she interpreted the four as the four orienting functions of consciousness: thinking, feeling, sensation, intuition. She noticed, however, that the four were all alike, whereas the four functions are all unlike. This raised no question for her, but it did for me. What are these four if they are *not* the four functional aspects of consciousness? I doubted whether this could be a sufficient interpretation of them. They seemed to be much more than that, and that is probably the reason why they are not different but identical. They do not form four functions, different by definition, but they might well represent the *a priori* possibility for the formation of the four functions. In this picture we have the quaternity, the archetypal 4, which is capable of numerous interpretations, as history shows and as I have demonstrated elsewhere. It illustrates the coming to consciousness of an un-

---

[92] In Taoist philosophy, movement to the right means a "falling" life-process, as the spirit is then under the influence of the feminine *p'o*-soul, which embodies the *yin* principle and is by nature passionate. Its designation as the anima (cf. my "Commentary on *The Secret of the Golden Flower*," pars. 57ff.) is psychologically correct, although this touches only one aspect of it. The *p'o*-soul entangles *hun*, the spirit, in the world-process and in reproduction. A leftward or backward movement, on the other hand, means the "rising" movement of life. A "deliverance from outward things" occurs and the spirit obtains control over the anima. This idea agrees with my findings, but it does not take account of the fact that a person can easily have the spirit outside and the anima inside.
[93] This was told to me by the Rimpoche of Bhutia Busty, Sikkim.

Fig. 4. Neolithic relief from Tarxien, Malta
The spirals represent vine tendrils.

conscious content; hence it frequently occurs in cosmogonic myths. What is the precise significance of the fact that the four eddies are apparently turning to the left, when the division of the mandala into four denotes a process of becoming conscious, is a point about which I would rather not speculate. I lack the necessary material. Blue means air or pneuma, and the leftward movement an intensification of the unconscious influence. Possibly this should be taken as a pneumatic compensation for the strongly emphasized red colour, which signifies affectivity.

566   The mandala itself is bright red, but the four eddies have in the main a cool, greenish-blue colour, which the patient associated with "water." This might hang together with the leftward movement, since water is a favourite symbol for the unconscious.[94] The green of the circle in the middle signifies life in the chthonic sense. It is the "benedicta viriditas" of the alchemists.

567   The problematical thing about this picture is the fact that the black snake is outside the totality of the symbolic circle. In order to make the totality actual, it ought really to be inside. But if we remember the unfavourable significance of the snake, we shall understand why its assimilation into the symbol of psychic wholeness presents certain difficulties. If our conjecture about the leftward movement of the four eddies is correct, this would denote a trend towards the deep and dark side of the spirit,[95] by means of which the black snake could be assimilated. The snake, like the devil in Christian theology, represents the shadow, and one which goes far beyond anything personal and could therefore best be compared with a principle, such as the principle of evil.[96] It is the colossal shadow thrown by man, of which our age had to have such a devastating experience. It is no easy matter to fit this shadow into our cosmos. The view that we can simply turn our back on evil and in this way eschew it belongs to the long list of antiquated naïveties. This is sheer ostrich policy and does not affect the reality of evil in the slight-

[94] Water also symbolizes the "materiality" of the spirit when it has become a "fixed" doctrine. One is reminded, too, of the blue-green colour in Böhme, signifying "Liberty."

[95] For the double nature of the spirit (Mercurius duplex of the alchemists) see "The Phenomenology of the Spirit in Fairytales," supra.

[96] Cf. the fiery serpent of Lucifer in Böhme.

est. Evil is the necessary opposite of good, without which there would be no good either. It is impossible even to think evil out of existence. Hence the fact that the black snake remains outside expresses the critical position of evil in our traditional view of the world.[97]

568   The background of the picture is pale, the colour of parchment. I mention this fact in particular, as the pictures that follow show a characteristic change in this respect.

Picture 6

569   The background of Picture 6 is a cloudy grey. The mandala itself is done in the vividest colours, bright red, green, and blue. Only where the red outer membrane enters the blue-green nucleus does the red deepen to blood colour and the pale blue to a dark ultramarine. The wings of Mercury, missing in the previous picture, reappear here at the neck of the blood-red pistons (as previously on the neck of the black snake in Picture 4). But the most striking thing is the appearance of a swastika, undoubtedly wheeling to the right. (I should add that these pictures were painted in 1928 and had no direct connection with contemporary fantasies, which at that time were still unknown to the world at large.) Because of its green colour, the swastika suggests something plantlike, but at the same time it has the wavelike character of the four eddies in the previous picture.

570   In this mandala an attempt is made to unite the opposites red and blue, outside and inside. Simultaneously, the rightward movement aims at bringing about an ascent into the light of consciousness, presumably because the background has become noticeably darker. The black snake has disappeared, but has begun to impart its darkness to the entire background. To compensate this, there is in the mandala an upwards movement towards the light, apparently an attempt to rescue consciousness from the darkening of the environment. The picture was associated with a dream that occurred a few days before. Miss X dreamt that *she returned to the city after a holiday in the country. To her astonishment she found a tree growing in the middle of the room where she worked. She thought: "Well, with its thick bark this tree can withstand the heat of an apart-*

97 Cf. "A Psychological Approach to the Dogma of the Trinity," pars. 243ff.

ment." Associations to the tree led to its maternal significance. The tree would explain the plant motif in the mandala, and its sudden growth represents the higher level or freeing of consciousness induced by the movement to the right. For the same reason the "philosophical" tree is a symbol of the alchemical *opus*, which as we know is an individuation process.

571   We find similar ideas in Justin's gnosis. The angel Baruch stands for the pneuma of Elohim, and the "motherly" angel Naas for the craftiness of Edem. But both angels, as I have said, were also trees: Baruch the tree of life, Naas the tree of knowledge. Their division and polarity are in keeping with the spirit of the times (second–third centuries A.D.). But in those days, too, they knew of an individuation process, as we can see from Hippolytus.[98] Elohim, we are told, set the "prophet" Heracles the task of delivering the "Father" (the pneuma) from the power of the twelve wicked angels. This resulted in his twelve labours. Now the Heracles myth has in fact all the characteristic features of an individuation process: the journeys to the four directions,[99] four sons, submission to the feminine principle (Omphale) that symbolizes the unconscious, and the self-sacrifice and rebirth caused by Deianeira's robe.

572   The "thick bark" of the tree suggests the motif of protection, which appears in the mandala as the "formation of skins" (see par. 576). This is expressed in the motif of the protective black bird's wings, which shield the contents of the mandala from outside influences. The piston-shaped prolongations of the peripheral red substance are phallic symbols, indicating the entry of affectivity into the pneumatic interior. They are obviously meant to activate and enrich the spirit dwelling within. This "spirit" has of course nothing to do with intellect, rather with something that we would have to call spiritual substance (pneuma) or—in modern terms—"spiritual life." The underlying symbolical thought is no doubt the same as the view developed in the Clementine Homilies, that πνεῦμα (spirit) and σῶμα (body) are one in God.[100] The mandala, though only a symbol of the self as the psychic totality, is at the same time a God-image, for the central point, circle, and quaternity are

[98] *Elenchos*, V, 26, 27ff.

[99] *Psychology and Alchemy*, par. 457.

[100] Hauck, *Realencyclopädie für protestantische Theologie*, IV, p. 173, li. 59.

well-known symbols for the deity. The impossibility of distinguishing empirically between "self" and "God" leads, in Indian theosophy, to the identity of the personal and suprapersonal Purusha-Atman. In ecclesiastical as in alchemical literature the saying is often quoted: "God is an infinite circle (or sphere) whose centre is everywhere and the circumference nowhere." [101] This idea can be found in full development as early as Parmenides. I will cite the passage, because it alludes to the same motifs that underlie our mandala: "For the narrower rings [102] were filled with unmixed Fire, and those next to them with Night, but between these rushes the portion of Flame. And in the centre of these is the goddess [103] who guides everything; for throughout she rules over cruel Birth and Mating, sending the female to mate with the male, and conversely again the male with the female." [104]

573   The learned Jesuit, Nicholas Caussin, apropos the report in Clement of Alexandria that, on certain occasions, wheels were rolled round in the Egyptian temples,[105] comments that Democritus of Abdera called God νοῦν ἐν πυρὶ σφαιροειδεῖ [106] (*mentem in igne orbiculari,* 'mind in the spherical fire'). He goes on: "This was the view also of Parmenides, who defined God as στεφάνην,

101 Baumgartner (*Die Philosophie des Alanus de Insulis,* II, Part 4, p. 118) traces this saying to a *liber Hermetis* or *liber Trismegisti,* Cod. Par. 6319 and Cod. Vat. 3060.

102 Στεφάναι = *coronae.*

103 Δαίμων ἢ πάντα κυβέρναι, a feminine *daemonium.*

104 Freeman, *Ancilla to the Pre-Socratic Philosophers,* p. 45.

105 *Writings of Clement of Alexandria,* trans. by Wilson, II, p. 248: "Also Dionysius Thrax, the grammarian, in his book *Respecting the Exposition of the Symbolical Signification of Circles,* says expressly, 'Some signified actions not by words only, but also by symbols: . . . as the wheel that is turned in the temples of the gods [by] the Egyptians, and the branches that are given to the worshippers. For the Thracian Orpheus says:

> For the works of mortals on earth are like branches,
> Nothing has but one fate in the mind, but all things
> Revolve in a circle, nor is it lawful to abide in one place,
> But each keeps its own course wherewith it began.' "

[Verses translated from the Overbeck version in German quoted by the author.— TRANS.]

106 Diels, *Fragmente der Vorsokratiker,* II, p. 102. Aetius, *De plac. phil.,* I, 7, 16.

'crown,' a circle consisting of glowing light.[107] And it has been very clearly established by Iamblichus, in his book on the mysteries, that the Egyptians customarily represent God, the Lord of the world, as sitting in the lotus, a water-plant, the fruits as well as the leaves of which are round,[108] thereby indicating the circular motion of the mind, which everywhere returns into itself." This is also the origin, he says, of the ritual transformations or circuits ("circuitiones") that imitate the motion of the heavens. But the Stoics named the heavens a "round and revolving God" (*rotundum et volubilem Deum*). Caussin says it is to this that the "mystical" (*mystice* = symbolical) explanation of Psalm 12 : 8 refers: "In circuitu impii ambulant" (the ungodly wander in a circle); [109] they only walk round the periphery without ever reaching the centre, which is God. Here I would mention the wheel motif in mandala symbolism only in passing, as I have dealt with it in detail elsewhere.[110]

Picture 7

574   In Picture 7 it has indeed turned to night: the entire sheet which the mandala is painted on is black. All the light is concentrated in the sphere. The colours have lost their brightness but have gained in intensity. It is especially striking that the black has penetrated as far as the centre, so that something of what we feared has already occurred: the blackness of the snake and of the sombre surroundings has been assimilated by the nucleus and, at the same time, as the picture shows, is compensated by a golden light radiating out from the centre. The rays form an equal-armed cross, to replace the swastika of the previous picture, which is here represented only by four hooks

---

107 A reference to Cicero, *De natura deorum* (trans. by Rackham, p. 31): "Parmenides . . . invents a purely fanciful something resembling a crown—*stephane* is his name for it—an unbroken ring of glowing lights encircling the sky, which he entitles god; but no one can imagine this to possess divine form, or sensation." This ironic remark of Cicero's shows that he was the child of another age, already very far from the primordial images.

108 There are innumerable representations of the sun-child sitting in the lotus. Cf. Erman, *Die Religion der Aegypter*, p. 62 and *Handbook of Egyptian Religion*, p. 26. It is also found on Gnostic gems [*Psychology and Alchemy*, fig. 52]. The lotus is the customary seat of the gods in India.

109 [Or, as in the DV, "The wicked walk round about."—EDITORS.]

110 *Psychology and Alchemy*, pars. 214f.

suggesting a rightwards rotation. With the attainment of absolute blackness, and particularly its presence in the centre, the upward movement and rightward rotation seem to have come to an end. On the other hand, the wings of Mercury have undergone a noticeable differentiation, which presumably means that the sphere has sufficient power to keep itself afloat and not sink down into total darkness. The golden rays forming the cross bind the four together.[111] This produces an inner bond and consolidation as a defence against destructive influences [112] emanating from the black substance that has penetrated to the centre. For us the cross symbol always has the connotation of *suffering*, so we are probably not wrong in assuming that the mood of this picture is one of more or less painful *suspension*—remember the wings!—over the dark abyss of inner loneliness.

575   Earlier, I mentioned Böhme's lightning that "makes a cross," and I brought this cross into connection with the four elements. As a matter of fact, John Dee symbolizes the elements by an equal-armed cross.[113] As we said, the cross with a little circle in it is the alchemical sign for copper (*cuprum*, from Kypris, Aphrodite), and the sign for Venus is ♀. Remarkably enough, ⊕ is the old apothecary's sign for *spiritus Tartari* (tartaric acid), which, literally translated, means 'spirit of the underworld.' ⊕ is also the sign for red hematite (bloodstone). Hence there seems to be not only a cross that comes from above, as in Böhme's case and in our mandala, but also one that comes from below. In other words, the lightning—to keep to Böhme's image—can come from below out of the blood, from Venus or from Tartarus. Böhme's neutral "Salniter" is identical with salt in general, and one of the signs for this is ⊕. One can hardly imagine a better sign for the arcane substance, which salt was

---

111 This interpretation was confirmed for me by my Tibetan mentor, Lingdam Gomchen, abbot of Bhutia Busty: the swastika, he said, is that which "cannot be broken, divided, or spoilt." Accordingly, it would amount to an inner consolidation of the mandala.

112 Cf. the similar motif in the mandala of the *Amitāyur-dhyāna Sūtra*, in "The Psychology of Eastern Meditation," pars. 917, 930.

113 "Monas hieroglyphica," *Theatr. chem.* (1602), II, p. 220. Dee also associates the cross with fire.

considered to be by the sixteenth- and seventeenth-century alchemists. Salt, in ecclesiastical as well as alchemical usage, is the symbol for Sapientia and also for the distinguished or elect *personality*, as in Matthew 5 : 13: "Ye are the salt of the earth."

576   The numerous wavy lines or layers in the mandala could be interpreted as representing the formation of *layers of skin*, giving protection against outside influences. They serve the same purpose as the inner consolidation. These cortices probably have something to do with the dream of the tree in the workroom, which had a "thick bark." The formation of skins is also found in other mandalas, and it denotes a hardening or sealing off against the outside, the production of a regular rind or "hide." It is possible that this phenomenon would account for the cortices or *putamina* ('shards') mentioned in the cabala.[114] "For such is the name for that which abides outside holiness," such as the seven fallen kings and the four Achurayim.[115] From them come the "klippoth" or cortices. As in alchemy, these are the scoriae or slag, to which adheres the quality of plurality and of death. In our mandala the cortices are boundary lines marking off the inner unity and protecting it against the outer blackness with its disintegrating influences, personified by the snake.[116] The same motif is expressed by the petals of the lotus and by the skins of the onion: the outer layers are withered and desiccated, but they protect the softer, inner layers. The lotus seat of the Horus-child, of the Indian divinities, and of

---

[114] [Cf. "Answer to Job," *Psychology and Religion*, par. 595, n. 8.—EDITORS.]

[115] The seven kings refer to previous aeons, "perished" worlds, and the four Achurayim are the so-called "back of God": "All belong to Malkhuth; which is so called because it is last in the system of Aziluth . . . they exist in the depths of the Shekinah" (*Kabbala Denudata*, I, p. 72). They form a masculine-feminine quaternio "of the Father and Mother of the highest, and of the Senex Israel and Tebhunah" (I, p. 675). The Senex is Ain-Soph or Kether (I, p. 635), Tebhunah is Binah, intelligence (I, p. 726). The shards also mean unclean spirits.

[116] *Kabbala Denudata*, I, pp. 675f. The shards also stand for evil. (*Zohar*, I, 137aff., II, 34b.). According to a Christian interpretation from the 17th century, Adam Belial is the body of the Messiah, the "entire body or the host of shards." (Cf. II Cor. 6 : 15.) In consequence of the Fall, the host of shards irrupted into Adam's body, its outer layers being more infected than the inner ones. The "Anima Christi" fought and finally destroyed the shards, which signify matter. In connection with Adam Belial the text refers to Proverbs 6 : 12: "A naughty person, a wicked man, walketh with a froward mouth" (AV). (*Kabbala Denudata*, II, Appendix, cap. IX, sec. 2, p. 56.)

the Buddha must be understood in this sense. Hölderlin makes use of the same image:

> Fateless, like the sleeping
> Infant, breathe the heavenly ones,
> Chastely guarded
> In modest bud; their spirits
> Blossom eternally . . .[117]

577 In Christian metaphor, Mary is the flower in which God lies hidden; or again, the rose window in which the *rex gloriae* and judge of the world is enthroned.

578 The idea of circular layers is to be found, by implication, in Böhme, for the outermost ring of his three-dimensional mandala [118] is labelled "will of ye Devill Lucifer," "Abysse (of) Eternity," "Abyss of ye Darkness," "Hell of Devills," etc. (See Fig. 1.) Böhme says of this in his *Aurora* (ch. XVII, sec. 6): "Behold, when Lucifer with his hosts aroused the Wrath-fire in God's nature, so that God waxed wroth in Nature in the place of Lucifer, the outermost Birth in Nature acquired another Quality, wholly wrathful, dry, cold, vehement, bitter, and sour. The raging Spirit, that before had a subtle, gentle Quality in Nature, became in his outermost Birth wholly presumptuous and terrible, and now in his outermost Birth is called the Wind, or the element Air." In this way the four elements arose—the earth, in particular, by a process of contraction and desiccation.

579 Cabalistic influences may be conjectured here, though Böhme knew not much more about the Cabala than did Paracelsus. He regarded it as a species of magic. The four elements correspond to the four Achurayim.[119] They constitute a sort of

---

117 "Hyperion's Song of Fate," in *Gedichte*, p. 315. (Trans. as in Jung, *Symbols of Transformation*, p. 399.)

118 Concerning the total vision of the "Life of Spirit and Nature," Böhme says: "We may then liken it to a round spherical Wheel, which goes on all sides, as the Wheel in Ezekiel shows" (*Mysterium pansophicum*, Sämmtliche Werke, ed. Schiebler, VI, p. 416).

119 *Quaestiones Theosophicae* (Amsterdam edn., 1682), p. 23. *Aurora*, XVII. 9, p. 168, mentions the "seven Spirits, which kindled themselves in their outermost Birth or Geniture." They are the Spirits of God, "Source-Spirits" of eternal and timeless Nature, corresponding to the seven planets and forming the "Wheel of the Centre" (*Sig. rer.*, IX, 8ff., p. 60). These seven Spirits are the seven above-mentioned "Qualities" which all come from one mother. She is the "twofold

second quaternity, proceeding from the inner, pneumatic quaternity but of a physical nature. The alchemists, too, allude to the Achurayim. Mennens,[120] for instance, says: "And although the holy name of God reveals the Tetragrammaton or the Four Letters, yet if you should look at it aright, only three Letters are found in it. The letter *he* [ה] is found twice, since they are the same, namely Air and Water, which signifies the Son; Earth the Father, and Fire the Holy Ghost. Thus the Four Letters of God's name manifestly signify the Most Holy Trinity and Matter, which likewise is threefold (*triplex*) [121] . . . and which is also called the shadow of the same [i.e., of God], and is named by Moyses [122] the back of God [*Dei posteriora*], which seems to be created out of it [matter]." [123] This statement bears out Böhme's view.

580 To return to our mandala. The original four eddies have coalesced into the wavy squares in the middle of the picture. Their place is taken by golden points at the outer rim (developed from the previous picture), emitting rainbow colours. These are the colours of the *peacock's eye*, which play a great role as the *cauda pavonis* in alchemy.[124] The appearance of these

---

Source, evil and good in all things" (*Aurora*, p. 27). Cf. the "goddess" in Parmenides and the two-bodied Edem in Justin's gnosis.

120 Gulielmus Mennens (1525–1608), a learned Flemish alchemist, wrote a book entitled *Aurei velleris, sive sacrae philosophiae, naturae et artis admirabilium libri tres* (Antwerp, 1604). Printed in *Theatr. chem.*, V (1622), pp. 267ff.

121 "As therefore God is three and one, so also the matter from which he created all things is triplex and one." This is the alchemical equivalent of the conscious and unconscious triads of functions in psychology. Cf. also "The Phenomenology of the Spirit in Fairytales," pars. 425 and 436ff.

122 Mennens seems to refer not to the Cabala direct, but to a text ascribed to Moses, which I have not been able to trace. It is certainly not a reference to the Greek text called by Berthelot "Chimie de Moise" (*Alch. grecs*, IV, xxii). Moses is mentioned now and then in the old literature, and Lenglet du Fresnoy (*Histoire de la philosophie hermétique*, 1742, III, p. 22) cites under No. 26 a MS from the Vienna Bibliothek entitled: "Moysis Prophetae et Legislatoris Hebraeorum secretum Chimicum" (Ouvrage supposé).

123 "Aurei velleris," I, cap. X, in *Theatr. chem.*, V, pp. 334f.

124 The *cauda pavonis* is identified by Khunrath with Iris, the "nuncia Dei." Dorn ("De transmutatione metallorum," *Theatr. chem.*, I, p. 599) explains it as follows: "This is the bird which flies by night without wings, which the early dew of heaven, continually acting by upward and downward ascent and descent, turns into the head of a crow (*caput corvi*), then into the tail of a peacock, and

colours in the *opus* represents an intermediate stage preceding the definitive end result. Böhme speaks of a "love-desire or a Beauty of Colours; and here all Colours arise." [125] In our mandala, too, the rainbow colours spring from the red layer that means affectivity. Of the "life of Nature and Spirit" that is united in the "spherical wheel" [126] Böhme says: "Thus is made known to us an eternal Essence of Nature, like to Water and Fire, which stand as it were mixed into one another. For there comes a *bright-blue* colour, like the *Lightning* of the Fire; and then it has a form like a *Ruby* [127] mingled with Crystals into one Essence, or like *yellow, white, red,* and *blue* mingled in *dark Water:* for it is like blue in green, since each still has its brightness and shines, and the Water only resists their Fire, so that there is no wasting anywhere, but one eternal Essence in two Mysteries mingled together, notwithstanding the difference of two Principles, viz. two kinds of life." The phenomenon of the colours owes its existence to the "Imagination of the great Mystery, where a wondrous essential Life is born." [128]

---

afterwards it acquires the bright wings of a swan, and lastly an extreme redness, an index of its fiery nature." In Basilides (Hippolytus, *Elenchos*, X, 14, 1) the peacock's egg is synonymous with the *sperma mundi*, the κόκκος σινάπεως. It contains the "fullness of colours," 365 of them. The golden colour should be produced from the peacock's eggs, we are told in the Cyranides (Delatte, *Textes latins et vieux français relatifs aux Cyranides*, p. 171). The light of Mohammed has the form of a peacock, and the angels were made out of the peacock's sweat (Aptowitzer, "Arabisch-Jüdische Schöpfungstheorien," pp. 209, 233).

125 *Sig. rer.*, XIV, 10ff., pp. 112f.

126 See n. 118.

127 The carbuncle is a synonym for the *lapis*. "The king bright as a carbuncle" (Lilius, an old source in the "Rosarium philosophorum," *Art. aurif.*, 1593, II, p. 329). "A ray . . . in the earth, shining in the darkness after the manner of a carbuncle gathered into itself" (from Michael Maier's exposition of the theory of Thomas Aquinas, in *Symbola aureae mensae*, p. 377). "I found a certain stone, red, shining, transparent, and brilliant, and in it I saw all the forms of the elements and also their contraries" (quotation from Thomas in Mylius, *Philosophia reformata*, p. 42). For heaven, gold, and carbuncle as synonyms for the *rubedo*, see ibid., p. 104. The *lapis* is "shimmering carbuncle light" (Khunrath, *Von hyleal. Chaos*, p. 237). Ruby or carbuncle is the name for the *corpus glorificatum* (Glauber, *Tractatus de natura salium*, Part I, p. 42). In Rosencreutz's *Chemical Wedding* (1616) the bed-chamber of Venus is lit by carbuncles (p. 97). Cf. what was said above about *anthrax* (ruby and cinnabar).

128 *Mysterium pansophicum*, pp. 416f.

581   It is abundantly clear from this that Böhme was preoccupied with the same psychic phenomenon that fascinated Miss X—and many other patients too. Although Böhme took the idea of the *cauda pavonis* and the tetrameria from alchemy,[129] he, like the alchemists, was working on an empirical basis which has since been rediscovered by modern psychology. There are products of active imagination, and also dreams, which reproduce the same patterns and arrangements with a spontaneity that cannot be influenced. A good example is the following dream: A patient dreamt that *she was in a drawing-room. There was a table with* three chairs *beside it. An unknown man standing beside her invited her to sit down. For this purpose she fetched a* fourth *chair that stood further off. She then sat at the table and began turning over the pages of a book, containing pictures of* blue *and* red *cubes, as for a building game. Suddenly it occurred to her that she had something else to attend to. She left the room and went to a* yellow *house. It was raining in torrents, and she sought shelter under a* green *laurel tree.*

582   The table, the three chairs, the invitation to sit down, the other chair that had to be fetched to make four chairs, the cubes, and the building game all suggest a process of *composition*. This takes place in stages: a combination first of blue and red, then of yellow and green. These four colours symbolize four qualities, as we have seen, which can be interpreted in various ways. Psychologically this quaternity points to the orienting functions of consciousness, of which at least one is unconscious and therefore not available for conscious use. Here it would be the green, the sensation function,[130] because the patient's relation to the real world was uncommonly complicated and clumsy. The "inferior" function, however, just because of its unconsciousness, has the great advantage of being contaminated with the collective unconscious and can be used as a bridge to span the gulf between conscious and unconscious and thus restore the vital connection with the latter. This is the deeper reason why the dream represents the inferior function as a laurel. The laurel in this dream has the same connection with

129 The chemical causes of the *cauda pavonis* are probably the iridiscent skin on molten metals and the vivid colours of certain compounds of mercury and lead. These two metals were often used as the primary material.

130 Statistically, at least, green is correlated with the sensation function.

the processes of inner growth as the tree that Miss X dreamt grew in her room. It is essentially the same tree as the *arbor philosophica* of the alchemists, about which I have written in *Psychology and Alchemy*.[131] We should also remember that, according to tradition, the laurel is not injured either by lightning or by cold—"intacta triumphat." Hence it symbolized the Virgin Mary,[132] the model for all women, just as Christ is the model for men. In view of its historical interpretation the laurel, like the alchemical tree, should be taken in this context as a symbol of the self.[133] The ingenuousness of patients who produce such dreams is always very impressive.

583   To turn back again to our mandala. The golden lines that end in pistons recapitulate the spermatozoon motif and therefore have a spermatic significance, suggesting that the quaternity will be reproduced in a new and more distinct form. In so far as the quaternity has to do with conscious realization, we can infer from these symptoms an intensification of the latter, as is also suggested by the golden light radiating from the centre. Probably a kind of inner illumination is meant.

584   Two days before painting this picture, Miss X dreamt that *she was in her father's room in their country house. "But my mother had moved my bed away from the wall into the middle of the room and had slept in it. I was furious, and moved the bed back to its former place. In the dream the bed-cover was red—exactly the red reproduced in the picture."*

585   The mother significance of the tree in her previous dream has here been taken up by the unconscious: this time the mother has slept in the middle of the room. This seems to be for Miss X an annoying intrusion into her sphere, symbolized by the room of her father, who has an animus significance for her. Her sphere is therefore a spiritual one, and she has usurped it just as she usurped her father's room. She has thus identified with the "spirit." Into this sphere her mother has intruded and installed herself in the centre, at first under the symbol of the

---

131 [See the index, s.v.; also Jung, "The Philosophical Tree."—EDITORS.]

132 "Lovely laurel, evergreen in all its parts, standing midmost among many trees smitten by lightning, bears the inscription: 'Untouched it triumphs.' This similitude refers to Mary the Virgin, alone among all creatures undefiled by any lightning-flash of sin." Picinelli, *Mondo simbolico* (1669), Lib. IX, cap. XVI.

133 Cf. "The Spirit Mercurius," par. 241.

tree. She therefore stands for physis opposed to spirit, i.e., for the natural feminine being which the dreamer also is, but which she would not accept because it appeared to her as a black snake. Although she remedied the intrusion at once, the dark chthonic principle, the black substance, has nevertheless penetrated to the centre of her mandala, as Picture 7 shows. But just because of this the golden light can appear: "e tenebris lux!" We have to relate the mother to Böhme's idea of the matrix. For him the matrix is the *sine qua non* of all differentiation or realization, without which the spirit remains suspended and never comes down to earth. The collision between the paternal and the maternal principle (spirit and nature) works like a shock.

586   After this picture, she felt the renewed penetration of the red colour, which she associated with feeling, as something disturbing, and she now discovered that her "rapport" with me, her analyst (= father), was unnatural and unsatisfactory. She was giving herself airs, she said, and was posing as an intelligent, understanding pupil (usurpation of spirituality!). But she had to admit that she felt very silly and was very silly, regardless of what I thought about it. This admission brought her a feeling of great relief and helped her to see at last that sex was "not, on the one hand, merely a mechanism for producing children and not, on the other, only an expression of supreme passion, but was also banally physiological and autoerotic." This belated realization led her straight into a fantasy state where she became conscious of a series of obscene images. At the end she saw the image of a large bird, which she called the "earth bird," and which alighted on the earth. Birds, as aerial beings, are well-known spirit symbols. It represented the transformation of the "spiritual" image of herself into a more earthy version that is more characteristic of women. This "tailpiece" confirms our suspicion that the intensive upward and rightward movement has come to a halt: the bird is coming down to earth. This symbolization denotes a further and necessary differentiation of what Böhme describes in general as "Love-desire." Through this differentiation consciousness is not only widened but also brought face to face with the reality of things, so that the inner experience is tied, so to speak, to a definite spot.

587   On the days following, the patient was overcome by feelings of self-pity. It became clear to her how much she regretted never having had any children. She felt like a neglected animal or a lost child. This mood grew into a regular *Weltschmerz*, and she felt like the "all-compassionate Tathagata" (Buddha). Only when she had completely given way to these feelings could she bring herself to paint another picture. Real liberation comes not from glossing over or repressing painful states of feeling, but only from experiencing them to the full.

Picture 8

588   The thing that strikes us at once in Picture 8 is that almost the whole interior is filled with the black substance. The blue-green of the water has condensed to a dark blue quaternity, and the golden light in the centre turns in the reverse direction, anti-clockwise: the bird is coming down to earth. That is, the mandala is moving towards the dark, chthonic depths. It is still floating—the wings of Mercury show this—but it has come much closer to the blackness. The inner, undifferentiated quaternity is balanced by an outer, differentiated one, which Miss X equated with the four functions of consciousness. To these she assigned the following colours: yellow = intuition, light blue = thinking, flesh pink = feeling, brown = sensation.[134] Each of these quarters is divided into three, thus producing the number 12 again. The separation and characterization of the two quaternities is worth noting. The outer quaternity of wings appears as a differentiated realization [135] of the undifferentiated inner one, which really represents the archetype. In the cabala this relationship corresponds to the quaternity of Merkabah [136] on the one hand and of the Achurayim on the other, and in Böhme they are the four Spirits of God [137] and the four elements.

---

134 The colour correlated with sensation in the mandalas of other persons is usually green.   135 Cf. the Achurayim quaternity.

136 Chochmah (= face of the man), Binah (= eagle), Gedulah (= lion), Gebhurah (= bull), the four symbolical angels in Ezekiel's vision.

137 He gives them the names of planets and describes them as the "four Bailiffs, who hold government in the Mother, the Birth-giver." They are Jupiter, Saturn, Mars, and Sun. "In these four Forms the Spirit's Birth consists, viz. the true Spirit both in the inward and outward Being" (*Sig. rer.*, IX, 9ff., p. 61).

589   The plantlike form of the cross in the middle of the mandala, also noted by the patient, refers back to the tree ("tree of the cross") and the mother.[138] She thus makes it clear that this previously taboo element has been accepted and now holds the central place. She was fully conscious of this—which of course was a great advance on her previous attitude.

590   In contrast to the previous picture there are no inner cortices. This is a logical development, because the thing they were meant to exclude is now in the centre, and defence has become superfluous. Instead, the cortices spread out into the darkness as golden rings, expanding concentrically like waves. This would mean a far-reaching influence on the environment emanating from the sealed-off self.

591   Four days before she painted this mandala she had the following dream: *"I drew a young man to the window and, with a brush dipped in white oil, removed a black fleck from the cornea of his eye. A little golden lamp then became visible in the centre of the pupil. The young man felt greatly relieved, and I told him he should come again for treatment. I woke up saying the words: 'If therefore thine eye be single, thy whole body shall be full of light.'"* (Matthew 6 : 22.)

592   This dream describes the change: the patient is no longer identical with her animus. The animus has, so to speak, become *her* patient, since he has eye trouble. As a matter of fact the animus usually sees things "cock-eyed" and often very unclearly. Here a black fleck on the cornea obscures the golden light shining from inside the eye. He has "seen things too blackly." The eye is the prototype of the mandala, as is evident from Böhme, who calls his mandala "The Philosophique Globe, or Eye of ye Wonders of Eternity, or Looking-Glass of Wisdom." He says: "The substance and Image of the Soul may be resembled to the Earth, having a fair Flower growing out of it, and also to the Fire and Light; as we see that Earth is a Centre, but no life; yet it is essential, and a fair flower grows out of it, which is not like Earth . . . and yet the Earth is the Mother of the Flower." The soul is a "fiery Eye, and similitude of the First Principle," a "Centre of Nature." [139]

138 The connection between tree and mother, especially in Christian tradition, is discussed at length in *Symbols of Transformation*, Part II.
139 *A Summary Appendix of the Soul*, p. 117.

593   Our mandala is indeed an "eye," the structure of which symbolizes the centre of order in the unconscious. The eye is a hollow sphere, black inside, and filled with a semi-liquid substance, the vitreous humour. Looking at it from outside, one sees a round, coloured surface, the iris, with a dark centre, from which a golden light shines. Böhme calls it a "fiery eye," in accordance with the old idea that seeing emanates from the eye. The eye may well stand for consciousness (which is in fact an organ of perception), looking into its own background. It sees its own light there, and when this is clear and pure the whole body is filled with light. Under certain conditions consciousness has a purifying effect. This is probably what is meant by Matthew 6 : 22ff., an idea expressed even more clearly in Luke 11 : 33ff.

594   The eye is also a well-known symbol for God. Hence Böhme calls his "Philosophique Globe" the "Eye of Eternity," the "Essence of all Essences," the "Eye of God." [140]

595   By accepting the darkness, the patient has not, to be sure, changed it into light, but she has kindled a light that illuminates the darkness within. By day no light is needed, and if you don't know it is night you won't light one, nor will any light be lit for you unless you have suffered the horror of darkness. This is not an edifying text but a mere statement of the psychological facts. The transition from Picture 7 to Picture 8 gives one a working idea of what I mean by "accepting the dark principle." It has sometimes been objected that nobody can form a clear conception of what this means, which is regrettable, because it is an ethical problem of the first order. Here, then, is a practical example of this "acceptance," and I must leave it to the philosophers to puzzle out the ethical aspects of the process. [141]

---

140 *Forty Questions*, pp. 24ff.

141 I do not feel qualified to go into the ethics of what "venerable Mother Nature" has to do in order to unfold her precious flower. Some people can, and those whose temperament makes them feel an ethical compulsion must do this in order to satisfy a need that is also felt by others. Erich Neumann has discussed these problems in a very interesting way in his *Depth Psychology and a New Ethic*. It will be objected that my respect for Nature is a very unethical attitude, and I shall be accused of shirking "decisions." People who think like this evidently know all about good and evil, and why and for what one has to decide. Unfortunately I do not know all this so precisely, but I hope for my patients and for myself that everything, light and darkness, decision and agonizing doubt, may turn to "good"—and by "good" I mean a development such as

Picture 9

596 In Picture 9 we see for the first time the blue "soul-flower," on a red background, also described as such by Miss X (naturally without knowledge of Böhme).[142] In the centre is the golden light in the form of a lamp, as she herself stated. The cortices are very pronounced, but they consist of light (at least in the upper half of the mandala) and radiate outwards.[143] The light is composed of the rainbow hues of the rising sun; it is a real *cauda pavonis*. There are six sets of sunbeams. This recalls the Buddha's Discourse on the Robe, from the Collection of the Pali Canon:

His heart overflowing with lovingkindness . . . with compassion . . . with joyfulness . . . with equanimity, he abides, raying forth lovingkindness, compassion, joyfulness, equanimity, towards one quarter of space, then towards the second, then towards the third, then towards the fourth, and above and below, thus, all around. Everywhere, into all places the wide world over, his heart overflowing with compassion streams forth, wide, deep, illimitable, free from enmity, free from all ill-will. . . .[144]

597 But a parallel with the Buddhist East cannot be carried through here, because the mandala is divided into an upper and a lower half.[145] Above, the rings shine many-hued as a rainbow; below, they consist of brown earth. Above, there hover three white birds (*pneumata* signifying the Trinity); below, a goat

---

is here described, an unfolding which does no damage to either of them but conserves the possibilities of life.

142 *The Secret of the Golden Flower* had not been published then. Picture 9 was reproduced in it.

143 Cf. *Kabbala Denudata*, Appendix, ch. IV, sec. 2, p. 26: "The beings created by the infinite Deity through the First Adam were all spiritual beings, viz. they were simple, shining acts, being one in themselves, partaking of a being that may be thought of as the midpoint of a sphere, and partaking of a life that may be imagined as a sphere emitting rays."

144 "Parable of the Cloth," in *The First Fifty Discourses from the Collection of the Middle-Length Discourses (Majjhima Nikaya) of Gotama the Buddha*, I, pp. 39f., modified. This reference to the Buddha is not accidental, since the figure of the Tathagata in the lotus seat occurs many times in the patient's mandalas.

145 Tibetan mandalas are not so divided, but very often they are embedded between heaven and hell, i.e., between the benevolent and the wrathful deities.

is rising up, accompanied by two ravens (Wotan's birds)[146] and twining snakes. This is not the sort of picture a Buddhist holy man would make, but that of a Western person with a Christian background, whose light throws a dark shadow. What is more, the three birds float in a jet black sky, and the goat, rising out of dark clay, is shown against a field of bright orange. This, oddly enough, is the colour of the Buddhist monk's robe, which was certainly not a conscious intention of the patient. The underlying thought is clear: no white without black, and no holiness without the devil. Opposites are brothers, and the Oriental seeks to liberate himself from them by his *nirdvandva* ("free from the two") and his *neti neti* ("not this, not that"), or else he puts up with them in some mysterious fashion, as in Taoism. The connection with the East is deliberately stressed by the patient, through her painting into the mandala four hexagrams from the *I Ching*.[147]

598   The sign in the left top half is "Yü, ENTHUSIASM" (No. 16). It means "Thunder comes resounding out of the earth," i.e., a movement coming from the unconscious, and expressed by music and dancing. Confucius comments as follows:

Firm as a rock, what need of a whole day?
The judgment can be known.
The superior man knows what is hidden and what is evident.
He knows weakness, he knows strength as well.
Hence the myriads look up to him.
Enthusiasm can be the source of beauty, but it can also delude.

599   The second hexagram at the top is "Sun, DECREASE" (No. 41). The upper trigram means Mountain, the lower trigram means Lake. The mountain towers above the lake and "restrains" it. That is the "image" whose interpretation points to self-restraint and reserve, i.e., a seeming decrease of oneself. This is significant in the light of "ENTHUSIASM." In the top line of the hexagram, "But [one] no longer has a separate home," the homelessness of the Buddhist monk is meant. On the psychological level this does not, of course, refer to so drastic a

---

[146] This is the lower triad that corresponds to the Trinity, just as the devil is occasionally depicted with three heads. Cf. also "Phenomenology of the Spirit in Fairytales," pars. 425 and 436ff.
[147] Trans. by Wilhelm and Baynes (1967), pp. 67ff.

600   demonstration of renunciation and independence, but to the patient's irreversible insight into the conditioned quality of all relationships, into the relativity of all values, and the transience of all things.

601   The sign in the bottom half to the right is "Sheng, PUSHING UPWARD" (No. 46). "Within the earth, wood grows: The image of Pushing Upward." It also says: "One pushes upward into an empty city," and "The king offers him Mount Ch'i." So this hexagram means growth and development of the personality, like a plant pushing out of the earth—a theme already anticipated by the plant motif in an earlier mandala. This is an allusion to the important lesson which Miss X has learnt from her experience: that there is no development unless the shadow is accepted.

601   The hexagram to the left is "Ting, THE CAULDRON" (No. 50). This is a bronze sacrificial vessel equipped with handles and legs, which held the cooked viands used for festive occasions. The lower trigram means Wind and Wood, the upper one Fire. The "Cauldron" is thus made up of "fire over wood," just as the alchemical vessel consists of fire or water.[148] There is "delicious food" in it (the "fat of the pheasant"), but it is not eaten because "the handle of the *ting* is altered" and its "legs are broken," making it unusable. But, as a result of "constant self-abnegation," the personality becomes differentiated ("the *ting* has golden carrying rings" and even "rings of jade") and purified, until it acquires the "hardness and soft lustre" of precious jade.[149]

602   Though the four hexagrams were put into the mandala on purpose, they are authentic results of preoccupation with the *I Ching*. The phases and aspects of my patient's inner process of development can therefore express themselves easily in the language of the *I Ching*, because it too is based on the psychology of the individuation process that forms one of the main interests of Taoism and of Zen Buddhism.[150] Miss X's interest in Eastern philosophy was due to the deep impression which a better knowledge of her life and of herself had made upon her—an

---

[148] *Psychology and Alchemy*, par. 338.
[149] The same idea as the transformation into the *lapis*. Cf. ibid., par. 378.
[150] Good examples are *The Secret of the Golden Flower* and Suzuki, *Introduction to Zen Buddhism*.

impression of the tremendous contradictions in human nature. The insoluble conflict she was faced with makes her preoccupation with Eastern therapeutic systems, which seem to get along without conflict, doubly interesting. It may be partly due to this acquaintance with the East that the opposites, irreconcilable in Christianity, were not blurred or glossed over, but were seen in all their sharpness, and in spite (or perhaps just because) of this, were brought together into the unity of the mandala. Böhme was never able to achieve this union; on the contrary, in his mandala the bright and dark semi-circles are turned back to back. The bright half is labelled "H. Ghost," the dark half "Father," i.e., *auctor rerum* [151] or "First Principle," whereas the Holy Ghost is the "Second Principle." This polarity is crossed by the paired opposites "Sonne" and "Earthly Man." The "Devills" are all on the side of the dark "Father" and constitute his "Wrath-fire," just as on the periphery of the mandala.

603   Böhme's starting-point was philosophical alchemy, and to my knowledge he was the first to try to organize the Christian cosmos, as a total reality, into a mandala.[152] The attempt failed, inasmuch as he was unable to unite the two halves in a circle. Miss X's mandala, on the other hand, comprises and contains the opposites, as a result, we may suppose, of the support afforded by the Chinese doctrine of Yang and Yin, the two metaphysical principles whose co-operation makes the world go round. The hexagrams, with their firm (yang) and yielding (yin) lines, illustrate certain phases of this process. It is therefore right that they should occupy a mediating position between above and below. Lao-tzu says: "High stands on low." This indisputable truth is secretly suggested in the mandala: the three white birds hover in a black field, but the grey-black goat

151 Cf. the above quotation from the "Aureum vellus" of Mennens, where earth signifies the Father and his "shadow" signifies matter. Böhme's view is thoroughly consistent with the character of Yahweh, who, despite his role as the guardian of justice and morality, is amoral and unjust. Cf. Stade, *Biblische Theologie des Alten Testaments*, I, pp. 88f.

152 I am purposely disregarding the numerous arrangements in a circle such as the *rex gloriae* with the four evangelists, Paradise with its four rivers, the heavenly hierarchies of Dionysius the Areopagite, etc. These all ignore the reality of evil, because they regard it as a mere *privatio boni* and thereby dismiss it with a euphemism.

has a bright orange-coloured background. Thus the Oriental truth insinuates itself and makes possible—at least by symbolic anticipation—a union of opposites within the irrational life process formulated by the *I Ching*. That we are really concerned here with opposite phases of one and the same process is shown by the picture that now follows.

Picture 10

604   In Picture 10, begun in Zurich but only completed when Miss X again visited her motherland, we find the same division as before into above and below. The "soul-flower" [153] in the centre is the same, but it is surrounded on all sides by a dark blue night sky, in which we see the four phases of the moon, the new moon coinciding with the world of darkness below. The three birds have become two. Their plumage has darkened, but on the other hand the goat has turned into two semi-human creatures with horns and light faces, and only two of the four snakes remain. A notable innovation is the appearance of two *crabs* in the lower, chthonic hemisphere that also represents the body. The crab has essentially the same meaning as the astrological sign Cancer.[154] Unfortunately Miss X gave no context here. In such cases it is usually worth investigating what use has been made in the past of the object in question. In earlier, prescientific ages hardly any distinction was drawn between long-tailed crabs (*Macrura*, crayfish) and short-tailed crabs (*Brachyura*). As a zodiacal sign Cancer signifies *resurrection,* because the crab sheds its shell.[155] The ancients had in mind chiefly *Pagurus bernhardus*, the hermit crab. It hides in its shell and cannot be attacked. Therefore it signifies *caution* and *foresight, knowledge of coming events.*[156] It "depends on the moon, and

---

153 Cf. Rahner, "Die seelenheilende Blume."

154 Cf. Bouché-Leclercq, *L'Astrologie grecque*, p. 136: Cancer = "crabe ou écrevisse." The constellation was usually represented as a tailless crab.

155 "The crab is wont to change with the changing seasons; casting off its old shell, it puts on a new and fresh one." This, says Picinelli, is an "emblema" of the resurrection of the dead, and cites Ephesians 4 : 23: ". . . be renewed in the spirit of your minds" (RSV). (*Mondo simbolico*, Lib. VI, No. 45.)

156 Foreseeing the flooding of the Nile, the crabs (like the tortoises and crocodiles) bring their eggs in safety to a higher place. "They foresee the future in their mind long before it comes." Caussin, *Polyhistor symbolicus* (1618), p. 442.

waxes with it." [157] It is worth noting that the crab appears just in the mandala in which we see the phases of the moon for the first time. Astrologically, Cancer is the house of the moon. Because of its backwards and sideways movement, it plays the role of an unlucky animal in superstition and colloquial speech ("crabbed," "catch a crab," etc.). Since ancient times cancer (καρκίνος) has been the name for a malignant tumour of the glands. Cancer is the zodiacal sign in which the sun begins to retreat, when the days grow shorter. Pseudo-Kallisthenes relates that crabs dragged Alexander's ships down into the sea.[158] "Karkinos" was the name of the crab that bit Heracles in the foot in his fight with the Lernaean monster. In gratitude, Hera set her accomplice among the stars.[159]

605   In astrology, Cancer is a feminine and watery sign,[160] and the summer solstice takes place in it. In the *melothesiae* [161] it is correlated with the *breast*. It rules over the *Western sea*. In Propertius it makes a sinister appearance: "Octipedis Cancri terga sinistra time" (Fear thou the ill-omened back of the eight-footed crab).[162] De Gubernatis says: "The crab . . . causes now the death of the solar hero and now that of the monster." [163] The *Panchatantra* (V, 2) relates how a crab, which the mother gave to her son as apotropaic magic, saved his life by killing a black snake.[164] As De Gubernatis thinks, the crab stands now for the sun and now for the moon,[165] according to whether it goes forwards or backwards.

606   Miss X was born in the first degrees of Cancer (actually about 3°). She knew her horoscope and was well aware of the significance of the moment of birth; that is, she realized that the degree of the rising sign (the ascendent) conditions the individuality of the horoscope. Since she obviously guessed the

---

157 Masenius, *Speculum imaginum veritatis occultae* (1714), cap. LXVII, 30, p. 768.   158 De Gubernatis, *Zoological Mythology*, II, p. 355.

159 Roscher, *Lexikon*, II, col. 959, s.v. "Karkinos." The same motif occurs in a dream described in *Two Essays on Analytical Psychology*, pars. 8off.

160 In Egypt, the heliacal rising of Cancer indicates the beginning of the annual flooding of the Nile and hence the beginning of the year. Bouché-Leclercq, p. 137.   161 [Cf. "Psychology and Religion," p. 67, n. 5.—EDITORS.]

162 Propertius, trans. by Butler, p. 275.   163 De Gubernatis, II, p. 356.

164 *The Panchatantra Reconstructed*, ed. by Edgerton, II, pp. 403f. Cf. also Hoffmann-Krayer et al., *Handwörterbuch des Deutschen Aberglaubens*, V, col. 448, s.v. "Krebs."   165 De Gubernatis, II, p. 356.

horoscope's affinity with the mandala, she introduced her individual sign into the painting that was meant to express her psychic self.[166]

607   The essential conclusion to be drawn from Picture 10 is that the dualities which run through it are always inwardly balanced, so that they lose their sharpness and incompatibility. As Multatuli says: "Nothing is quite true, and even that is not quite true." But this loss of strength is counterbalanced by the unity of the centre, where the lamp shines, sending out coloured rays to the eight points of the compass.[167]

608   Although the attainment of inner balance through symmetrical pairs of opposites was probably the main intention of this mandala, we should not overlook the fact that the *duplication motif* also occurs when unconscious contents are about to become conscious and differentiated. They then split, as often happens in dreams, into two identical or slightly different halves corresponding to the conscious and still unconscious aspects of the nascent content. I have the impression, from this picture, that it really does represent a kind of solstice or climax, where decision and division take place. The dualities are, at bottom, Yes and No, the irreconcilable opposites, but they *have* to be held together if the balance of life is to be maintained. This can only be done by holding unswervingly to the centre, where action and suffering balance each other. It is a path "sharp as the edge of a razor." A climax like this, where universal opposites clash, is at the same time a moment when a wide perspective often opens out into the past and future. This is the psychological moment when, as the *consensus gentium* has established since ancient times, synchronistic phenomena occur—that is, when the far appears near: sixteen years later, Miss X became fatally ill with cancer of the breast.[168]

[166] Her horoscope shows four earth signs but no air sign. The danger coming from the animus is reflected in ☽ ☐ ☿.
[167] Cf. the Buddhist conception of the "eight points of the compass" in the *Amitāyur-dhyāna Sūtra;* cf. "The Psychology of Eastern Meditation," pp. 560ff.
[168] I do not hesitate to take the synchronistic phenomena that underlie astrology seriously. Just as there is an eminently psychological reason for the existence of alchemy, so too in the case of astrology. Nowadays it is no longer interesting to know how far these two fields are aberrations; we should rather investigate the psychological foundations on which they rest. [Cf. Jung, "Synchronicity: An Acausal Connecting Principle," *passim.*—EDITORS.]

Picture 11

609   Here I will only mention that the coloured rays emanating from the centre have become so rarified that, in the next few pictures, they disappear altogether. Sun and moon are now outside, no longer included in the microcosm of the mandala. The sun is not golden, but has a dull, ochrous hue and in addition is clearly turning to the left: it is moving towards its own obscuration, as had to happen after the cancer picture (solstice). The moon is in the first quarter. The roundish masses near the sun are probably meant to be cumulus clouds, but with their grey-red hues they look suspiciously like bulbous swellings. The interior of the mandala now contains a quincunx of stars, the central star being silver and gold. The division of the mandala into an aerial and an earthy hemisphere has transferred itself to the outside world and can no longer be seen in the interior. The silvery rim of the aerial hemisphere in the preceding picture now runs round the entire mandala and recalls the band of quicksilver that, as *Mercurius vulgaris,* "veils the true personality." At all events, it is probable that the influence and importance of the outside world are becoming so strong in this picture as to bring about an impairment and devaluation of the mandala. It does not break down or burst (as can easily happen under similar circumstances), but is removed from the telluric influence through the symbolical constellation of stars and heavenly bodies.

Pictures 12–24

610   In Picture 12 the sun is in fact sinking below the horizon and the moon is coming out of the first quarter. The radiation of the mandala has ceased altogether, but the equivalents of sun and moon, and also of the earth, have been assimilated into it. A remarkable feature is its sudden inner animation by two human figures and various animals. The constellation character of the centre has vanished and given way to a kind of flower motif. What this animation means cannot be established, unfortunately, as we have no commentary.

611   In Picture 13 the source of radiation is no longer in the mandala but outside, in the shape of the full moon, from which

rings of rainbow-coloured light radiate in concentric circles. The mandala is laced together by four black and golden snakes, the heads of three of them pointing to the centre, while the fourth rears upwards. In between the snakes and the centre there are indications of the spermatozoon motif. This may mean an intensive penetration on the part of the outside world, but it could also mean magical protection. The breaking down of the quaternity into 3 plus 1 is in accord with the archetype.[169]

612   In Picture 14 the mandala is suspended over the lit-up ravine of Fifth Avenue, New York, whither Miss X in the meantime returned. On the blue flower in the centre the *coniunctio* of the "royal" pair is represented by the sacrificial fire burning between them. The King and Queen are assisted by two kneeling figures of a man and a woman. It is a typical marriage quaternio, and for an understanding of its psychology I must refer the reader to my account in the "Psychology of the Transference."[170] This inner bond should be thought of as a compensatory "consolidation" against disintegrating influences from without.

613   In Picture 15 the mandala floats between Manhattan and the sea. It is daylight again, and the sun is just rising. Out of the blue centre blue snakes penetrate into the red flesh of the mandala: the enantiodromia is setting in, after the introversion of feeling caused by the shock of New York had passed its climax. The blue colour of the snakes indicates that they have acquired a pneumatic nature.

614   From Picture 16 onwards, the drawing and painting technique shows a decided improvement. The mandalas gain in aesthetic value. In Picture 17 a kind of *eye motif* appears, which I have also observed in the mandalas of other persons. It seems to me to link up with the motif of *polyophthalmia* and to point to the peculiar nature of the unconscious, which can be regarded as a "multiple consciousness." I have discussed this question in detail elsewhere.[171] (See also Fig. 5.)

[169] An instance of the axiom of Maria. Other well-known examples are Horus and his 4 (or 3 + 1) sons, the 4 symbolical figures in Ezekiel, the 4 evangelists and—last but not least—the 3 synoptic gospels and the 1 gospel of St. John.
[170] [Ch. 2, pp. 211ff.—EDITORS.]
[171] "On the Nature of the Psyche," sec. 6.

Fig. 5. Mandala by a woman patient

Aged 58, artistic and technically accomplished. In the centre is the egg
encircled by the snake; outside, apotropaic wings and eyes. The
mandala is exceptional in that it has a pentadic structure. (The patient
also produced triadic mandalas. She was fond of playing with forms
irrespective of their meaning—a consequence of her artistic gift.)

615   The enantiodromia only reached its climax the following year, in Picture 19.[172] In that picture the red substance is arranged round the golden, four-rayed star in the centre, and the blue substance is pushing everywhere to the periphery. Here the rainbow-coloured radiation of the mandala begins again for the first time, and from then on was maintained for over ten years (in mandalas not reproduced here).

616   I will not comment on the subsequent pictures, nor reproduce them all—as I say, they extend over more than ten years—because I feel I do not understand them properly. In addition, they came into my hands only recently, after the death of the patient, and unfortunately without text or commentary. Under these circumstances the work of interpretation becomes very uncertain, and is better left unattempted. Also, this case was meant only as an example of how such pictures come to be produced, what they mean, and what reflections and observations their interpretation requires. It is not intended to demonstrate how an entire lifetime expresses itself in symbolic form. The individuation process has many stages and is subject to many vicissitudes, as the fictive course of the *opus alchymicum* amply shows.

Conclusion

617   Our series of pictures illustrates the initial stages of the way of individuation. It would be desirable to know what happens afterwards. But, just as neither the philosophical gold nor the philosophers' stone was ever made in reality, so nobody has ever been able to tell the story of the whole way, at least not to mortal ears, for it is not the story-teller but death who speaks the final "consummatum est." Certainly there are many things worth knowing in the later stages of the process, but, from the point of view of teaching as well as of therapy, it is important

---

172 [Pictures 18–24, which were not reproduced with the earlier versions of this essay, were chosen by Professor Jung from among those painted by the patient after the termination of analytical work. The dates of the entire series of pictures were as follows: 1–6, Oct. 1928; 7 9, Nov. 1928; 10, Jan.; 11, Feb.; 12, June; 13, Aug.; 14, Sept.; 15, Oct.; 16. 17, Nov., all 1929; 18, Feb. 1930; 19, Aug. 1930; 20, March 1931; 21, July 1933; 22. Aug. 1933 23, 1935; 24, "Night-blooming cereus, done May 1938, on last trip to Jung" (patient's notation).—EDITORS.]

not to skip too quickly over the initial stages. As these pictures are intuitive anticipations of future developments, it is worth while lingering over them for a long time, in order, with their help, to integrate so many contents of the unconscious into consciousness that the latter really does reach the stage it sees ahead. These psychic evolutions do not as a rule keep pace with the tempo of intellectual developments. Indeed, their very first goal is to bring a consciousness that has hurried too far ahead into contact again with the unconscious background with which it should be connected. This was the problem in our case too. Miss X had to turn back to her "motherland" in order to find her earth again—*vestigia retro!* It is a task that today faces not only individuals but whole civilizations. What else is the meaning of the frightful regressions of our time? The tempo of the development of consciousness through science and technology was too rapid and left the unconscious, which could no longer keep up with it, far behind, thereby forcing it into a defensive position which expresses itself in a universal will to destruction. The political and social isms of our day preach every conceivable ideal, but, under this mask, they pursue the goal of lowering the level of our culture by restricting or altogether inhibiting the possibilities of individual development. They do this partly by creating a chaos controlled by terrorism, a primitive state of affairs that affords only the barest necessities of life and surpasses in horror the worst times of the so-called "Dark" Ages. It remains to be seen whether this experience of degradation and slavery will once more raise a cry for greater spiritual freedom.

618   This problem cannot be solved collectively, because the masses are not changed unless the individual changes. At the same time, even the best-looking solution cannot be forced upon him, since it is a good solution only when it is combined with a natural process of development. It is therefore a hopeless undertaking to stake everything on collective recipes and procedures. The bettering of a general ill begins with the individual, and then only when he makes himself and not others responsible. This is naturally only possible in freedom, but not under a rule of force, whether this be exercised by a self-elected tyrant or by one thrown up by the mob.

619   The initial pictures in our series illustrate the characteristic psychic processes which set in the moment one gives a mind to that part of the personality which has remained behind, forgotten. Scarcely has the connection been established when symbols of the self appear, trying to convey a picture of the total personality. As a result of this development, the unsuspecting modern gets into paths trodden from time immemorial—the *via sancta*, whose milestones and signposts are the religions.[173] He will think and feel things that seem strange to him, not to say unpleasant. Apuleius relates that in the Isis mysteries he "approached the very gates of death and set one foot on Proserpina's threshold, yet was permitted to return, rapt through all the elements. At midnight I saw the sun shining as if it were noon; I entered the presence of the gods of the underworld and the gods of the upper world, stood near and worshipped them." [174] Such experiences are also expressed in our mandalas; that is why we find in religious literature the best parallels to the symbols and moods of the situations they formulate. These situations are intense inner experiences which can lead to lasting psychic growth and a ripening and deepening of the personality, if the individual affected by them has the moral capacity for πίστις, loyal trust and confidence. They are the age-old psychic experiences that underlie "faith" and ought to be its unshakable foundation—and not of faith alone, but also of knowledge.

620   Our case shows with singular clarity the spontaneity of the psychic process and the transformation of a personal situation into the problem of individuation, that is, of becoming whole, which is the answer to the great question of our day: How can consciousness, our most recent acquisition, which has bounded ahead, be linked up again with the oldest, the unconscious, which has lagged behind? The oldest of all is the instinctual foundation. Anyone who overlooks the instincts will be ambuscaded by them, and anyone who does not humble himself will be humbled, losing at the same time his freedom, his most precious possession.

621   Always when science tries to describe a "simple" life-process, the matter becomes complicated and difficult. So it is no wonder

[173] Isaiah 45 : 8: "And a highway shall be there, and it shall be called the Holy Way" (RSV).   [174] *The Golden Ass*, trans. by Graves, p. 286.

that the details of a transformation process rendered visible through active imagination make no small demands on our understanding. In this respect they may be compared with all other biological processes. These, too, require specialized knowledge to become comprehensible. Our example also shows, however, that this process can begin and run its course without any special knowledge having to stand sponsor to it. But if one wants to understand anything of it and assimilate it into consciousness, then a certain amount of knowledge is needed. If the process is not understood at all, it has to build up an unusual intensity so as not to sink back again into the unconscious without result. But if its affects rise to an unusual pitch, they will enforce some kind of understanding. It depends on the correctness of this understanding whether the consequences turn out more pathologically or less. Psychic experiences, according to whether they are rightly or wrongly understood, have very different effects on a person's development. It is one of the duties of the psychotherapist to acquire such knowledge of these things as will enable him to help his patient to an adequate understanding. Experiences of this kind are not without their dangers, for they are also, among other things, the matrix of the psychoses. Stiffnecked and violent interpretations should under all circumstances be avoided, likewise a patient should never be forced into a development that does not come naturally and spontaneously. But once it has set in, he should not be talked out of it again, unless the possibility of a psychosis has been definitely established. Thorough psychiatric experience is needed to decide this question, and it must constantly be borne in mind that the constellation of archetypal images and fantasies is not in itself pathological. The pathological element only reveals itself in the way the individual reacts to them and how he interprets them. The characteristic feature of a pathological reaction is, above all, *identification with the archetype*. This produces a sort of inflation and possession by the emergent contents, so that they pour out in a torrent which no therapy can stop. Identification can, in favourable cases, sometimes pass off as a more or less harmless inflation. But in all cases identification with the unconscious brings a weakening of consciousness, and herein lies the danger. You do not "make" an identification, you do not "identify yourself," but you experience your identity with the archetype in an unconscious way and so are possessed by it. Hence in more difficult cases it is far more necessary to strengthen and consolidate the ego than to understand and assimilate the products of the unconscious. The decision must be left to the diagnostic and therapeutic tact of the analyst.

*

622   This paper is a groping attempt to make the inner processes of the mandala more intelligible. They are, as it were, self-delineations of dimly sensed changes going on in the background, which are perceived by the "reversed eye" and rendered visible with pencil and brush, just as they are, uncomprehended and unknown. The pictures represent a kind of ideogram of unconscious contents. I have naturally used this method on myself too and can affirm that one can paint very complicated pictures without having the least idea of their real meaning. While painting them, the picture seems to develop out of itself and often in opposition to one's conscious intentions. It is interesting to observe how the execution of the picture frequently thwarts one's expectations in the most surprising way. The same thing can be observed, sometimes even more clearly, when writing down the products of active imagination.[175]

623   The present work may also serve to fill a gap I myself have felt in my exposition of therapeutic methods. I have written very little on active imagination, but have talked about it a great deal. I have used this method since 1916, and I sketched it out for the first time in "The Relations between the Ego and the Unconscious." I first mentioned the mandala in 1929, in *The Secret of the Golden Flower*.[176] For at least thirteen years I kept quiet about the results of these methods in order to avoid any suggestion. I wanted to assure myself that these things—mandalas especially—really are produced spontaneously and were not suggested to the patient by my own fantasy. I was then

---

[175] Case material in Meier, "Spontanmanifestationen des kollektiven Unbewussten," 284ff.; Bänziger, "Persönliches und Archetypisches im Individuationsprozess," p. 272; Gerhard Adler, *Studies in Analytical Psychology*, pp. 90ff.
[176] Active imagination is also mentioned in "The Aims of Psychotherapy," pars. 101ff. Cf. also "The Transcendent Function." For other pictures of mandalas see the next paper in the present vol.

able to convince myself, through my own studies, that mandalas were drawn, painted, carved in stone, and built, at all times and in all parts of the world, long before my patients discovered them. I have also seen to my satisfaction that mandalas are dreamt and drawn by patients who were being treated by psychotherapists whom I had not trained. In view of the importance and significance of the mandala symbol, special precautions seemed to be necessary, seeing that this motif is one of the best examples of the universal operation of an archetype. In a seminar on children's dreams, which I held in 1939–40,[177] I mentioned the dream of a ten-year-old girl who had absolutely no possibility of ever hearing about the quaternity of God. The dream was written down by the child herself and was sent to me by an acquaintance: *"Once in a dream I saw an animal that had lots of horns. It spiked up other little animals with them. It wriggled like a snake and that was how it lived. Then a blue fog came out of all the four corners, and it stopped eating. Then God came, but there were really four Gods in the four corners. Then the animal died, and all the animals it had eaten came out alive again."*

624   This dream describes an unconscious individuation process: all the animals are eaten by the one animal. Then comes the enantiodromia: the dragon changes into pneuma, which stands for a divine quaternity. Thereupon follows the apocatastasis, a resurrection of the dead. This exceedingly "unchildish" fantasy can hardly be termed anything but archetypal. Miss X, in Picture 12, also put a whole collection of animals into her mandala —two snakes, two tortoises, two fishes, two lions, two pigs, a goat and a ram.[178] Integration gathers many into one. To the child who had this dream, and to Miss X likewise, it was certainly not known that Origen had already said (speaking of the sacrificial animals): "Seek these sacrifices within thyself, and thou wilt find them within thine own soul. Understand that thou hast within thyself flocks of cattle . . . flocks of sheep and

177 [*Psychologische Interpretation von Kinderträumen*, winter semester, 1939–40, Federal Polytechnic Institute, Zurich (mimeographed stenographic record). The same dream is discussed by Dr. Jacobi in *Complex/Archetype/Symbol*, pp. 139ff.— Editors.]
178 One thinks here of a Noah's Ark that crosses over the waters of death and leads to a rebirth of all life.

flocks of goats. . . . Understand that the birds of the sky are also within thee. Marvel not if we say that these are within thee, but understand that thou thyself art even another little world, and hast within thee the sun and the moon, and also the stars." [179]

625   The same idea occurs again in another passage, but this time it takes the form of a psychological statement: "For look upon the countenance of a man who is at one moment angry, at the next sad, a short while afterward joyful, then troubled again, and then contented. . . . See how he who thinks himself one is not one, but seems to have as many personalities as he has moods, as also the Scripture says: A fool is changed as the moon. . . .[180] God, therefore, is unchangeable, and is called one for the reason that he changes not. Thus also the true imitator of God, who is made after God's image, is called one and the selfsame [unus et ipse] when he comes to perfection, for he also, when he is fixed on the summit of virtue, is not changed, but remains alway one. For every man, whiles he is in wickedness [malitia], is divided among many things and torn in many directions; and while he is in many kinds of evil he cannot be called one." [181]

626   Here the many animals are affective states to which man is prone. The individuation process, clearly alluded to in this passage, subordinates the many to the One. But the One is God, and that which corresponds to him in us is the *imago Dei*, the God-image. But the God-image, as we saw from Jakob Böhme, expresses itself in the mandala.

179 *In Leviticum Homiliae*, V, 2 (Migne, *P.G.*, vol. 12, col. 449).
180 Ecclesiasticus 27 : 11.
181 *In libros Regnorum homiliae*, I, 4 (Migne, *P.G.*, vol. 12, cols. 998–99).

CONCERNING MANDALA SYMBOLISM [1]

627   In what follows I shall try to describe a special category of symbols, the *mandala*, with the help of a wide selection of pictures. I have dealt with this theme on several occasions before, and in *Psychology and Alchemy* I gave a detailed account, with running commentary, of the mandala symbols that came up in the course of an individual analysis. I repeated the attempt in the preceding paper of the present volume, but there the mandalas did not derive from dreams but from active imagination. In this paper I shall present mandalas of the most varied provenance, on the one hand to give the reader an impression of the astonishing wealth of forms produced by individual fantasy, and on the other hand to enable him to form some idea of the regular occurrence of the basic elements.

628   As regards the interpretation, I must refer the reader to the literature. In this paper I shall content myself with hints, because a more detailed explanation would lead much too far, as the mandalas described in "Psychology and Religion" and in the preceding paper of this volume show.

629   The Sanskrit word *mandala* means 'circle.' It is the Indian term for the circles drawn in religious rituals. In the great temple of Madura, in southern India, I saw how a picture of this kind was made. It was drawn by a woman on the floor of the *mandapam* (porch), in coloured chalks, and measured about ten feet across. A pandit who accompanied me said in reply to my questions that he could give me no information about it. Only the women who drew such pictures knew what they

1 [First published, as "Über Mandalasymbolik," in *Gestaltungen des Unbewussten* (Psychologische Abhandlungen, VII; Zurich, 1950). The illustrations had originally .been collected for a seminar which Professor Jung gave at Berlin in 1930. Nine of them (Figs. 1, 6, 9, 25, 26, 28, 36, 37, 38) were published with brief comments as "Examples of European Mandalas" in *Das Geheimnis der goldenen Blüte*, by Jung and Richard Wilhelm (Munich, 1929; 2nd edn., Zurich, 1938), translated by C. F. Baynes as *The Secret of the Golden Flower* (London and New York, 1931; rev. edn., 1962); subsequently published in *Coll. Works*, vol. 13. In his *Memories, Dreams, Reflections* Jung acknowledged having painted the mandalas in Figs. 6 and 36 (thus also those in Figs. 28 and 29) and the frontispiece; see U.S. edn., pp. 197, 195; Brit. edn., pp. 188ff., 187.—EDITORS.]

meant. The woman herself was non-committal; she evidently did not want to be disturbed in her work. Elaborate mandalas, executed in red chalk, can also be found on the whitewashed walls of many huts. The best and most significant mandalas are found in the sphere of Tibetan Buddhism.[2] I shall use as an example a Tibetan mandala, to which my attention was drawn by Richard Wilhelm.

Figure 1

630   A mandala of this sort is known in ritual usage as a *yantra*, an instrument of contemplation. It is meant to aid concentration by narrowing down the psychic field of vision and restricting it to the centre. Usually the mandala contains three circles, painted in black or dark blue. They are meant to shut out the outside and hold the inside together. Almost regularly the outer rim consists of fire, the fire of *concupiscentia*, 'desire,' from which proceed the torments of hell. The horrors of the burial ground are generally depicted on the outer rim. Inside this is a garland of lotus leaves, characterizing the whole mandala as a *padma*, 'lotus-flower.' Then comes a kind of monastery court-yard with four gates. It signifies sacred seclusion and concentration. Inside this courtyard there are as a rule the four basic colours, red, green, white, and yellow, which represent the four directions and also the psychic functions, as the Tibetan Book of the Dead [3] shows. Then, usually marked off by another magic circle, comes the centre as the essential object or goal of contemplation.

631   This centre is treated in very different ways, depending on the requirements of the ritual, the grade of initiation of the contemplator, and the sect he belongs to. As a rule it shows Shiva in his world-creating emanations. Shiva, according to Tantric doctrine, is the One Existent, the Timeless in its perfect state. Creation begins when this unextended point—known as *Shiva-bindu*—appears in the eternal embrace of its feminine side, the Shakti. It then emerges from the state of being-in-itself and attains the state of being-for-itself, if I may use the Hegelian terminology.

2 Cf. *Psychology and Alchemy*, pars. 122ff.
3 [Cf. Jung, Psychological Commentary on the *Tibetan Book of the Dead*, par. 850.—EDITORS.]

632   In *kundalini* yoga symbolism, Shakti is represented as a snake wound three and a half times round the *lingam,* which is Shiva in the form of a phallus. This image shows the *possibility* of manifestation in space. From Shakti comes Maya, the building material of all individual things; she is, in consequence, the creatrix of the real world. This is thought of as illusion, as being and not-being. It *is,* and yet remains dissolved in Shiva. Creation therefore begins with an act of division of the opposites that are united in the deity. From their splitting arises, in a gigantic explosion of energy, the multiplicity of the world.

633   The goal of contemplating the processes depicted in the mandala is that the yogi shall become inwardly aware of the deity. Through contemplation, he recognizes himself as God again, and thus returns from the illusion of individual existence into the universal totality of the divine state.

634   As I have said, mandala means 'circle.' There are innumerable variants of the motif shown here, but they are all based on the squaring of a circle. Their basic motif is the premonition of a centre of personality, a kind of central point within the psyche, to which everything is related, by which everything is arranged, and which is itself a source of energy. The energy of the central point is manifested in the almost irresistible compulsion and urge to *become what one is,* just as every organism is driven to assume the form that is characteristic of its nature, no matter what the circumstances. This centre is not felt or thought of as the ego but, if one may so express it, as the *self.* Although the centre is represented by an innermost point, it is surrounded by a periphery containing everything that belongs to the self—the paired opposites that make up the total personality. This totality comprises consciousness first of all, then the personal unconscious, and finally an indefinitely large segment of the collective unconscious whose archetypes are common to all mankind. A certain number of these, however, are permanently or temporarily included within the scope of the personality and, through this contact, acquire an individual stamp as the shadow, anima, and animus, to mention only the best-known figures. The self, though on the one hand simple, is on the other hand an extremely composite thing, a "conglomerate soul," to use the Indian expression.

635   Lamaic literature gives very detailed instructions as to how such a circle must be painted and how it should be used. Form and colour are laid down by tradition, so the variants move within fairly narrow limits. The ritual use of the mandala is actually non-Buddhist; at any rate it is alien to the original Hīnayāna Buddhism and appears first in Mahāyāna Buddhism.

636   The mandala shown here depicts the state of one who has emerged from contemplation into the absolute state. That is why representation of hell and the horrors of the burial ground are missing. The diamond thunderbolt, the *dorje* in the centre, symbolizes the perfect state where masculine and feminine are united. The world of illusions has finally vanished. All energy has gathered together in the initial state.

637   The four *dorjes* in the gates of the inner courtyard are meant to indicate that life's energy is streaming inwards; it has detached itself from objects and now returns to the centre. When the perfect union of all energies in the four aspects of wholeness is attained, there arises a static state subject to no more change. In Chinese alchemy this state is called the "Diamond Body," corresponding to the *corpus incorruptibile* of medieval alchemy, which is identical with the *corpus glorificationis* of Christian tradition, the incorruptible body of resurrection. This mandala shows, then, the union of all opposites, and is embedded between *yang* and *yin,* heaven and earth; the state of everlasting balance and immutable duration.

638   For our more modest psychological purposes we must abandon the colourful metaphysical language of the East. What yoga aims at in this exercise is undoubtedly a psychic change in the adept. The ego is the expression of individual existence. The yogin exchanges his ego for Shiva or the Buddha; in this way he induces a shifting of the psychological centre of personality from the personal ego to the impersonal non-ego, which is now experienced as the real "Ground" of the personality.

639   In this connection I would like to mention a similar Chinese conception, namely the system on which the *I Ching* is based.

Figure 2

640   In the centre is *ch'ien,* 'heaven,' from which the four emanations go forth, like the heavenly forces extending through space. Thus we have:

74

ch'ien: self-generated creative energy, corresponding to Shiva.

heng: all-pervading power.

yuen: generative power.

li: beneficent power.

ching: unchangeable, determinative power.

641   Round this masculine power-centre lies the earth with its formed elements. It is the same conception as the Shiva-Shakti union in *kundalini* yoga, but here represented as the earth receiving into itself the creative power of heaven. The union of heaven with *kun,* the feminine and receptive, produces the *tetraktys,* which, as in Pythagoras, underlies all existence.

642   The "River Map" is one of the legendary foundations of the *I Ching,* which in its present form derives partly from the twelfth century B.C. According to the legend, a dragon dredged the magical signs of the "River Map" from a river. On it the sages discovered the drawing, and in the drawing the laws of the world-order. This drawing, in accordance with its extreme age, shows the knotted cords that signify numbers. These numbers have the usual primitive character of qualities, chiefly masculine and feminine. All uneven numbers are masculine, even numbers feminine.

643   Unfortunately I do not know whether this primitive conception influenced the formation of the much younger Tantric mandala. But the parallels are so striking that the European investigator has to ask himself: Which view influenced the other? Did the Chinese develop from the Indian, or the Indian from the Chinese? An Indian whom I asked answered: "Naturally the Chinese developed from the Indian." But he did not know how old the Chinese conceptions are. The bases of the *I Ching* go back to the third millennium B.C. My late friend Richard Wilhelm, the eminent expert on classical Chinese philosophy, was of the opinion that no direct connections could be assumed. Nor, despite the fundamental similarity of the symbolic ideas, does there need to be any direct influence, since the ideas, as experience shows and as I think I have demonstrated, arise autochthonously again and again, independently of one another, out of a psychic matrix that seems to be ubiquitous.

Figure 3

644   As a counterpart to the Lamaic mandala, I now reproduce the Tibetan "World Wheel," which should be sharply distinguished from the former, since it represents the world. In the centre are the three principles: cock, snake, and pig, symbolizing lust, envy, and unconsciousness. The wheel has, near the centre, six spokes, and twelve spokes round the edge. It is based on a triadic system. The wheel is held by the god of death, Yama. (Later we shall meet other "shield-holders": Figs. 34 and 47.) It is understandable that the sorrowful world of old age, sickness, and death should be held in the claws of the death-demon. The incomplete state of existence is, remarkably enough, expressed by a triadic system, and the complete (spiritual) state by a tetradic system. The relation between the incomplete and the complete state therefore corresponds to the "sesquitertian proportion" of 3 : 4. This relation is known in Western alchemical tradition as the axiom of Maria. It also plays a not inconsiderable role in dream symbolism.[4]

*

645   We shall now pass on to individual mandalas spontaneously produced by patients in the course of an analysis of the unconscious. Unlike the mandalas so far discussed, these are not based on any tradition or model, seeming to be free creations of fantasy, but determined by certain archetypal ideas unknown to their creators. For this reason the fundamental motifs are repeated so often that marked similarities occur in drawings done by the most diverse patients. The pictures come as a rule from educated persons who were unacquainted with the ethnic parallels. The pictures differ widely, according to the stage of the therapeutic process; but certain important stages correspond to definite motifs. Without going into therapeutic details, I would only like to say that a rearranging of the personality is involved, a kind of new centring. That is why mandalas mostly appear in connection with chaotic psychic states of disorientation or panic. They then have the purpose of reducing the confusion to order, though this is never the conscious intention

[4] Cf. the preceding paper, par. 552.

of the patient. At all events they express order, balance, and wholeness. Patients themselves often emphasize the beneficial or soothing effect of such pictures. Usually the mandalas express religious, i.e., numinous, thoughts and ideas, or, in their stead, philosophical ones. Most mandalas have an intuitive, irrational character and, through their symbolical content, exert a retroactive influence on the unconscious. They therefore possess a "magical" significance, like icons, whose possible efficacy was never consciously felt by the patient. In fact, it is from the effect of their own pictures that patients discover what icons can mean. Their pictures work not because they spring from the patients' own fantasy but because they are impressed by the fact that their subjective imagination produces motifs and symbols of the most unexpected kind that conform to law and express an idea or situation which their conscious mind can grasp only with difficulty. Confronted with these pictures, many patients suddenly realize for the first time the reality of the collective unconscious as an autonomous entity. I will not labour the point here; the strength of the impression and its effect on the patient are obvious enough from some of the pictures.

646   I must preface the pictures that now follow with a few remarks on the formal elements of mandala symbolism. These are primarily:

1. *Circular, spherical,* or *egg-shaped* formation.

2. The circle is elaborated into a *flower* (rose, lotus) or a *wheel.*

3. A centre expressed by a *sun, star,* or *cross,* usually with four, eight, or twelve rays.

4. The circles, spheres, and cruciform figures are often represented in *rotation* (swastika).

5. The circle is represented by a *snake* coiled about a centre, either ring-shaped (uroboros) or spiral (Orphic egg).

6. *Squaring of the circle,* taking the form of a circle in a square or vice versa.

7. *Castle, city,* and *courtyard* (*temenos*) motifs, quadratic or circular.

8. *Eye* (pupil and iris).

9. Besides the tetradic figures (and multiples of four), there are also triadic and pentadic ones, though these are much rarer.

They should be regarded as "disturbed" totality pictures, as we shall see below.

Figure 4

647   This mandala was done by a woman patient in her middle years, who first saw it in a dream. Here we see at once the difference from the Eastern mandala. It is poor in form, poor in ideas, but nevertheless expresses the individual attitude of the patient far more clearly than the Eastern pictures, which have been subjected to a collective and traditional configuration. Her dream ran: *"I was trying to decipher an embroidery pattern. My sister knew how. I asked her if she had made an elaborate hemstitched handkerchief. She said, "No, but I know how it was done." Then I saw it with the threads drawn, but the work not yet done. One must go around and around the square until near the centre, then go in circles."*

648   The spiral is painted in the typical colours red, green, yellow, and blue. According to the patient, the square in the centre represents a *stone,* its four facets showing the four basic colours. The inner spiral represents the snake that, like Kundalini, winds three and a half times [5] round the centre.

649   The dreamer herself had no notion of what was going on in her, namely the beginning of a new orientation, nor would she have understood it consciously. Also, the parallels from Eastern symbolism were completely unknown to her, so that any influence is out of the question. The symbolic picture came to her spontaneously, when she had reached a certain point in her development.

650   It is, unfortunately, not possible for me to say exactly under what circumstances each of these pictures arose. That would lead us too far. The sole aim of this paper is to give a survey of the formal parallels to the individual and collective mandala. I regret also that for the same reason no single picture can be interpreted circumstantially and in detail, as that would inevitably require a comprehensive account of the analytical situation of the patient. Wherever it is possible to shed light on the origins of the picture by a passing hint, as in the present case, I shall do so.

[5] The motif of $3\frac{1}{2}$ (the Apocalyptic number of days of affliction; cf. Rev. 11 : 9 and 11) refers to the alchemical dilemma "3 or 4?" or to the sesquitertian proportion (3 : 4). The *sesquitertius* is $3 + \frac{1}{3}$.

651   As to the interpretation of the picture, it must be emphasized that the snake, arranged in angles and then in circles
round the square, signifies the circumambulation of, and way
to, the centre. The snake, as a chthonic and at the same time
spiritual being, symbolizes the unconscious. The stone in the
centre, presumably a cube, is the quaternary form of the *lapis
philosophorum*. The four colours also point in this direction.[6]
It is evident that the stone in this case signifies the new centre
of personality, the self, which is also symbolized by a vessel.

Figure 5

652   The painter was a middle-aged woman of schizoid disposition. She had several times drawn mandalas spontaneously, because they always had an ordering effect on her chaotic psychic
states. The picture shows a rose, the Western equivalent of the
lotus. In India the lotus-flower (*padma*) is interpreted by the
Tantrists as the womb. We know this symbol from the numerous pictures of the Buddha (and other Indian deities) in the
lotus-flower.[7] It corresponds to the "Golden Flower" of Chinese
alchemy, the rose of the Rosicrucians, and the mystic rose in
Dante's *Paradiso*. Rose and lotus are usually arranged in groups
of four petals, indicating the squaring of the circle or the
united opposites. The significance of the rose as the maternal
womb was nothing strange to our Western mystics, for we read
in a prayer inspired by the Litany of Loreto:

O Rose-wreath, thy blossoming makes men weep for joy.
O rosy sun, thy burning makes men to love.
       O son of the sun,
       Rose-child,
       Sun-beam.
Flower of the Cross, pure Womb that blossoms
       Over all blooming and burning,
       Sacred Rose,
       Mary.

6 There is a very interesting American Indian parallel to this mandala: a white
snake coiled round a centre shaped like a cross in four colours. Cf. Newcomb
and Reichard, *Sandpaintings of the Navajo Shooting Chant*, Pl. XIII, pp. 13
and 78. The book contains a large number of interesting mandalas in colour.
7 The Egyptian Horus-child is likewise shown sitting in the lotus.

653   At the same time, the vessel motif is an expression of the content, just as Shakti represents the actualization of Shiva. As alchemy shows, the self is androgynous and consists of a masculine and a feminine principle. Conrad of Würzburg speaks of Mary, the flower of the sea in which Christ lies hidden. And in an old hymn we read:

> O'er all the heavens a rose appears
> And a bright dress of blossom wears.
> Its light glows in the Three-in-One
> For God himself has put it on.

Figure 6

654   The rose in the centre is depicted as a ruby, its outer ring being conceived as a wheel or a wall with gates (so that nothing can come out from inside or go in from outside). The mandala was a spontaneous product from the analysis of a male patient. It was based on a dream: *The dreamer found himself with three younger travelling companions in Liverpool.*[8] *It was night, and raining. The air was full of smoke and soot. They climbed up from the harbour to the "upper city."* The dreamer said: *"It was terribly dark and disagreeable, and we could not understand how anyone could stick it here. We talked about this, and one of my companions said that, remarkably enough, a friend of his had settled here, which astonished everybody. During this conversation we reached a sort of public garden in the middle of the city. The park was square, and in the centre was a lake or large pool. A few street lamps just lit up the pitch darkness, and I could see a little island in the pool. On it there was a single tree, a red-flowering magnolia, which miraculously stood in everlasting sunshine. I noticed that my companions had not seen this miracle, whereas I was beginning to understand why the man had settled here."*

655   The dreamer went on: "I tried to paint this dream. But as so often happens, it came out rather different. The magnolia turned into a sort of rose made of ruby-coloured glass. It shone like a four-rayed star. The square represents the wall of the park and at the same time a street leading round the park in a square. From it there radiate eight main streets, and from each

[8] Note the allusion in the name "Liver-pool." The liver is that which causes to live, the seat of life. [Cf. *Memories, Dreams, Reflections*, pp. 197f./195f.]

of these eight side-streets, which meet in a shining red central point, rather like the Étoile in Paris. The acquaintance mentioned in the dream lived in a house at the corner of one of these stars." The mandala thus combines the classic motifs of flower, star, circle, precinct (*temenos*), and plan of city divided into quarters with citadel. "The whole thing seemed like a window opening on to eternity," wrote the dreamer.

Figure 7

656   Flower motif with cross in the centre. The square, too, is arranged like a flower. The four faces at the corners correspond to the four cardinal points, which are often depicted as four deities. Here they have a demonic character. This may be connected with the fact that the patient was born in the Dutch East Indies, where she sucked up the peculiar local demonology with the mother's milk of her native ayah. Her numerous drawings all had a distinctly Eastern character, and thereby helped her to assimilate influences that at first could not be reconciled with her Western mentality.[9]

657   In the picture that followed, the demon faces were ornamentally elaborated in eight directions. For the superficial observer the flowerlike character of the whole may disguise the demonic element the mandala is meant to ward off. The patient felt that the "demonic" effect came from the European influence with its moralism and rationalism. Brought up in the East Indies until her sixth year, she came later into a conventional European milieu, and this had a devastating effect on the flowerlike quality of her Eastern spirit and caused a prolonged psychic trauma. Under treatment her native world, long submerged, came up again in these drawings, bringing with it psychic recovery.

Figure 8

658   The flowerlike development has got stronger and is beginning to overgrow the "demonishness" of the faces.

Figure 9

659   A later stage is shown here. Minute care in the draughtsmanship vies with richness of colour and form. From this we

9 [Cf. *The Practice of Psychotherapy*, 2nd edn., appendix, esp. par. 557.—EDITORS.]

can discern not only the extraordinary concentration of the patient but the triumph of Eastern "flowerlikeness" over the demon of Western intellectualism, rationalism, and moralism. At the same time the new centring of the personality becomes visible.

Figure 10

660   In this painting, done by another young woman patient, we see at the cardinal points four creatures: a bird, a sheep, a snake, and a lion with a human face. Together with the four colours in which the four regions are painted, they embody four principles. The interior of the mandala is empty. Or rather, it contains a "Nothing" that is expressed by a quaternity. This is in accord with the overwhelming majority of individual mandalas: as a rule the centre contains the motif of the *rotundum,* known to us from alchemy, or the four-fold emanation or the squaring of the circle, or—more rarely—the figure of the patient in a universal human sense, representing the Anthropos.[10] We find this motif, too, in alchemy. The four animals remind us of the cherubim in Ezekiel's vision, and also of the four symbols of the evangelists and the four sons of Horus, which are sometimes depicted in the same way, three with animal heads and one with a human head. Animals generally signify the instinctive forces of the unconscious, which are brought into unity within the mandala. This integration of the instincts is a prerequisite for individuation.

Figure 11

661   Painting by an older patient. Here the flower is seen not in the basic pattern of the mandala, but in elevation. The circular form has been preserved inside the square, so that despite its different execution this picture can still be regarded as a mandala. The plant stands for growth and development, like the green shoot in the diaphragm *chakra* of the *kundalini* yoga system. The shoot symbolizes Shiva and represents the centre and the male, whereas the calyx represents the female, the place of germination and birth.[11] Thus the Buddha sitting in the lotus is shown as the germinating god. It is the god in his rising,

10 [Cf. "Psychology and Religion," pars. 136f., 156f.]
11 [Cf. "The Philosophical Tree," par. 336 and fig. 27.—EDITORS.]

the same symbol as Ra the falcon, or the phoenix rising from the nest, or Mithras in the tree-top, or the Horus-child in the lotus. They are all symbolizations of the *status nascendi* in the seeding-place of the matrix. In medieval hymns Mary too is praised as the cup of the flower in which Christ, coming down as a bird, makes his nest. Psychologically Christ means unity, which clothes itself in the *corpus mysticum* of the Church or in the body of the Mother of God ("mystic rose"), surrounded as with flower-petals, and thus reveals itself in reality. Christ as an image is a symbol of the self.[12] Just as the plant stands for growth, so the flower depicts the unfolding from a centre.

Figure 12

662   Here the four rays emanating from the centre spread across the whole picture. This gives the centre a dynamic character. The structure of the flower is a multiple of four. The picture is typical of the marked personality of the patient, who had some artistic talent. (She also painted Fig. 5.) Besides that she had a strong feeling for Christian mysticism, which played a great role in her life. It was important for her to experience the archetypal background of Christian symbolism.

Figure 13

663   Photograph of a rug woven by a middle-aged woman, Penelope-like, at a time of great inner and outer distress. She was a doctor and she wove this magic circle round herself, working at it every day for months, as a counterbalance to the difficulties of her life. She was not my patient and could not have been influenced by me. The rug contains an eight-petalled flower. A special feature of the rug is that it has a real "above and below." Above is light; below, relative darkness. In it, there is a creature like a beetle, representing an unconscious content, and comparable with the sun in the form of Khepera. Occasionally the "above and below" are outside the protective circle, instead of inside. In that case the mandala affords protection against extreme opposites; that is, the sharpness of the conflict is not yet realized or else is felt as intolerable. The protective circle then guards against possible disruption due to the tension of opposites.

12 Cf. *Aion*, ch. 5.

Figure 14

664   An Indian picture of *Shiva-bindu,* the unextended point. It shows the divine power before the creation: the opposites are still united. The god rests in the point. Hence the snake signifies extension, the mother of Becoming, the creation of the world of forms. In India this point is also called Hiranyagarbha, 'golden germ' or 'golden egg.' We read in the Sanatsugatiya: "That pure great light which is radiant, that great glory which the gods worship, which makes the sun shine forth, that divine, eternal Being is perceived by the faithful." [13]

Figure 15

665   This picture, also by a middle-aged woman patient, shows the squaring of the circle. The plants again denote germination and growth. In the centre is a sun. As the snake-and-tree motif shows, we have here a conception of Paradise. A parallel is the Gnostic conception of Edem with the four rivers of Paradise in the Naassene gnosis. For the functional significance of the snake in relation to the mandala, see the preceding paper (comments on pictures 3, 4, and 5).

Figure 16

666   This picture was painted by a neurotic young woman. The snake is somewhat unusual in that it lies in the centre itself, its head coinciding with this. Usually it is outside the inner circle, or at least coiled round the central point. One suspects (rightly, as it turned out) that the inner darkness does not conceal the longed-for unity, the self, but rather the chthonic, feminine nature of the patient. In a later picture the mandala bursts and the snake comes out.

Figure 17

667   The picture was done by a young woman. This mandala is "legitimate" in so far as the snake is coiled round the four-rayed middle point. It is trying to get out: it is the awakening of Kundalini, meaning that the patient's chthonic nature is becoming active. This is also indicated by the arrows pointing

[13] *Sacred Books of the East,* VIII, p. 186, modified.

outwards. In practice it means becoming conscious of one's instinctual nature. The snake in ancient times personified the spinal ganglia and the spinal cord. Arrows pointing outwards may in other cases mean the opposite: protection of the inside from danger.

Figure 18

668   Drawn by an older patient. Unlike the previous picture, this one is "introverted." The snake is coiled round the four-rayed centre and has laid its head on the white, central point (*Shiva-bindu*), so that it looks as if it were wearing a halo. There seems to be a kind of incubation of the middle point—the motif of the snake guarding the treasure. The centre is often characterized as the "treasure hard to attain." [14]

Figure 19

669   Done by a middle-aged woman. The concentric circles express concentration. This is further emphasized by the fishes circumnavigating the centre. The number 4 has the meaning of total concentration. The movement to the left presumably indicates movement towards the unconscious, i.e., immersion in it.

Figure 20

670   This is a parallel to Figure 19: sketch of a fish-motif which I saw on the ceiling of the Maharajah's pavilion in Benares.

Figure 21

671   A fish instead of a snake. Fish and snake are simultaneously attributes of both Christ and the devil. The fish is making a whirlpool in the sea of the unconscious, and in its midst the precious pearl is being formed. A Rig-Veda hymn says:

> Darkness there was, concealed in darkness,
> A lightless ocean lost in night.
> Then the One, that was hidden in the shell,
> Was born through the power of fiery torment.
> From it arose in the beginning love,
> Which is the germ and the seed of knowledge.[15]

14 Cf. *Symbols of Transformation*, Part II, ch. 7.
15 Rig-Veda, X, 129, from Deussen trans., I, p. 123.

672   As a rule the snake personifies the unconscious, whereas the fish usually represents one of its contents. These subtle distinctions must be borne in mind when interpreting a mandala, because the two symbols very probably correspond to two different stages of development, the snake representing a more primitive and more instinctual state than the fish, which in history as well was endowed with higher authority than the snake (cf. the Ichthys-symbol).

Figure 22

673   In this picture by a young woman the fish has produced a differentiated centre by circumnavigation, and in it a mother and child stand before a stylized Tree of Life or of Knowledge. Here the fish has a dragonlike nature; it is a monster, a sort of Leviathan, which, as the texts from Ras Shamra show, was originally a snake.[16] Once more the movement is to the left.

Figure 23

674   The golden ball corresponds to the golden germ (Hiranyagarbha). It is rotating, and the Kundalini winding round it has doubled. This indicates conscious realization, since a content rising out of the unconscious splits at a certain moment into two halves, a conscious and an unconscious one. The doubling is not made by the conscious mind, but appears spontaneously in the products of the unconscious. The rightwards rotation, expressed by the wings (swastika-motif), likewise indicates conscious realization. The stars show that the centre has a cosmic structure. It has four rays, and thus behaves like a heavenly body. The Shatapatha-Brahmana says:

> Then he looks up to the sun, for that is the final goal, that the safe resort. To that final goal, to that resort he goes; for this reason he looks up to the sun.
> He looks up, saying, "Self-existent art thou, the best ray of light!" The sun is indeed the best ray of light, and therefore he says, "Self-existent art thou, the best ray of light!" "Light-bestowing art thou: give me light (varkas)!" "So say I," said Yajñavalkya, "and for this indeed the Brahmin should strive, if he would be brahma-varkasin, illumined by brahma."
> He then turns from left to right, saying, "I move along the course

16 [Cf. *Aion,* pars. 181f.—EDITORS.]

Figure 1

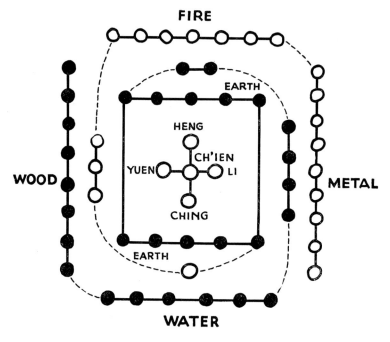

Figure 2

Figure 3

Figure 4

Figure 5

Figure 6

Figure 7

Figure 8

Figure 9

Figure 10

Figure 11

Figure 12

Figure 13

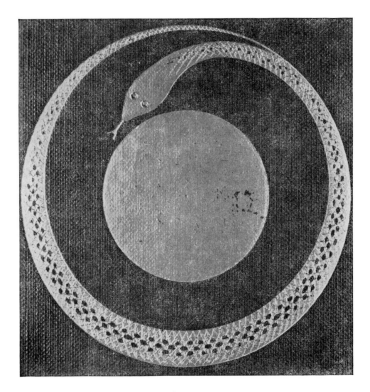

Figure 14

Figure 15

Figure 16

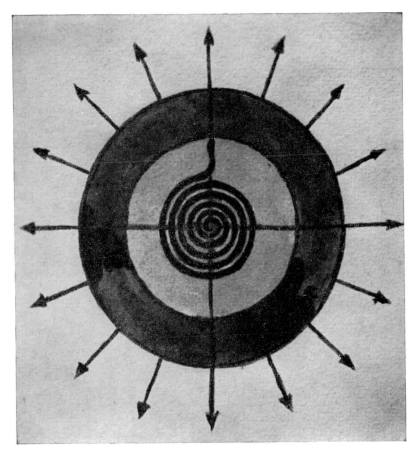

Figure 17

Figure 18

Figure 19

Figure 20

Figure 21

Figure 22

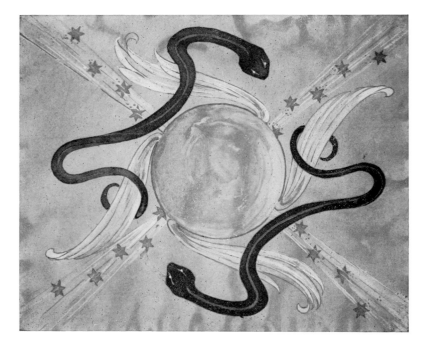

Figure 23

Figure 24

Figure 25

Figure 26

Figure 27

Figure 28

Figure 29

Figure 30

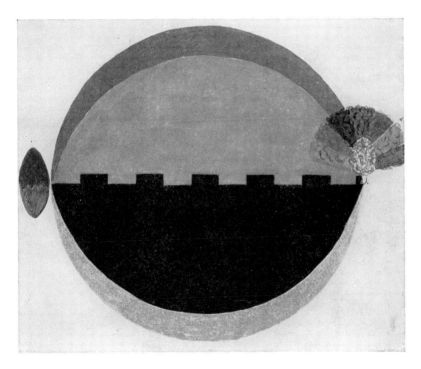

Figure 31

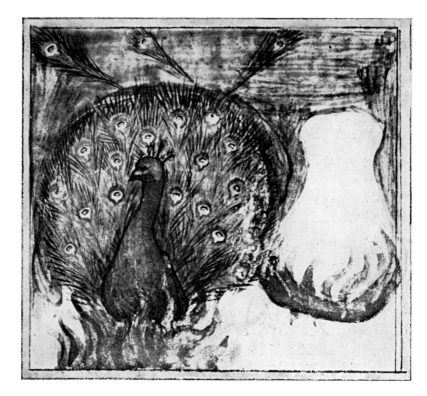

Figure 32

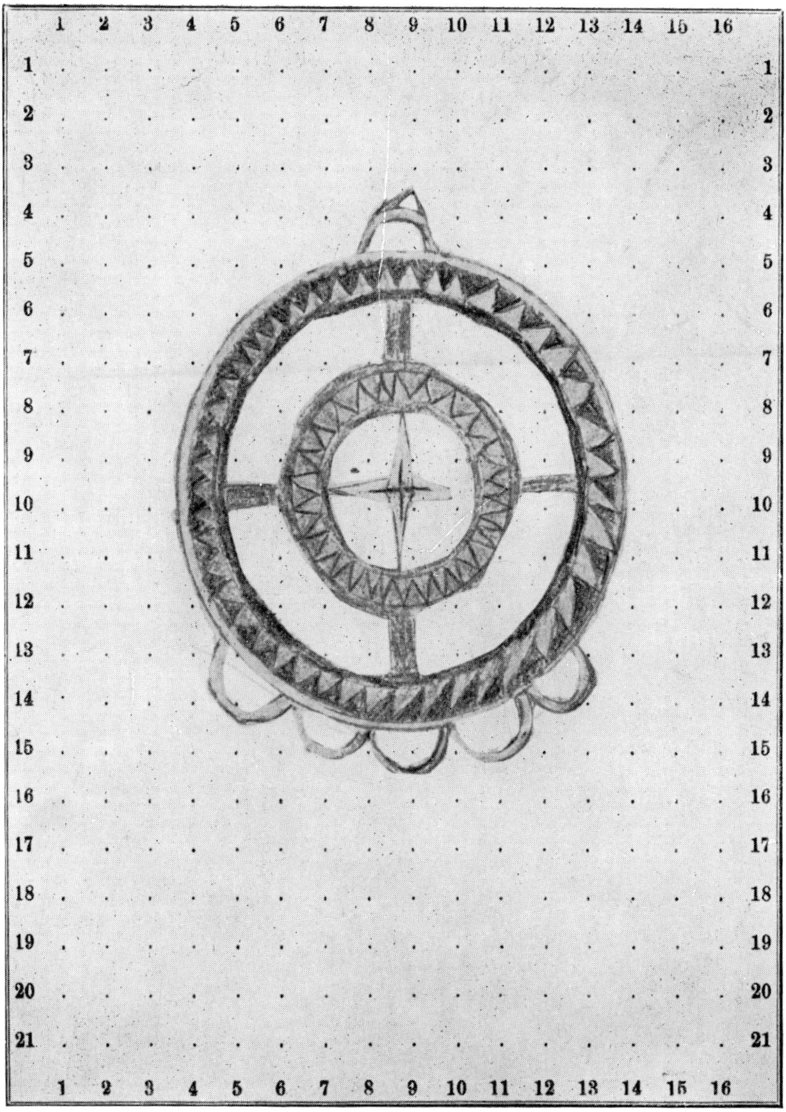
1 2 3 4 5 6 7 8 9 10 11 12 13 14 15 16
1
2
3
4
5
6
7
8
9
10
11
12
13
14
15
16
17
18
19
20
21
1 2 3 4 5 6 7 8 9 10 11 12 13 14 15 16

Figure 33

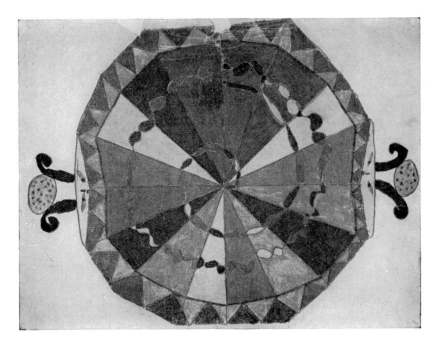

Figure 34

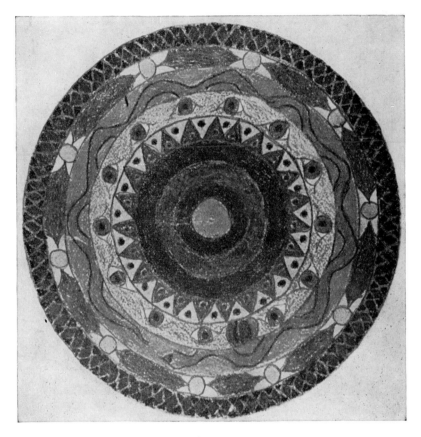

Figure 35

Figure 36

Figure 37

Figure 38

Figure 39

Figure 40

Figure 41

Figure 42

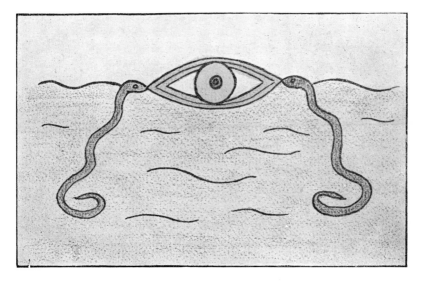

Figure 43

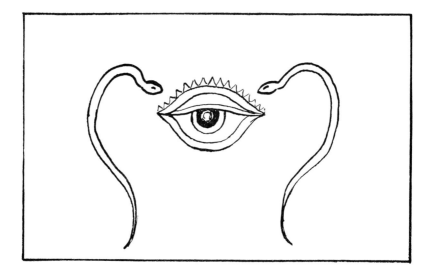

Figure 44

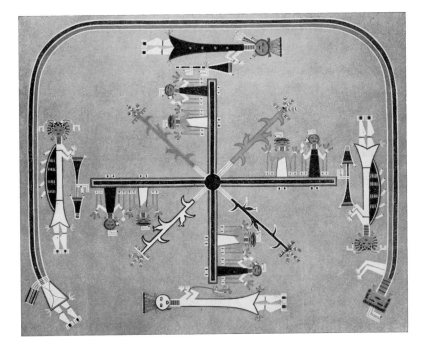

Figure 45

Figure 46

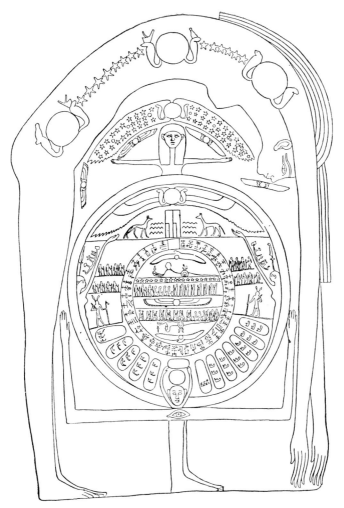

Figure 47

Figure 48

Figure 49

DECIMA FIGURA.

Figure 50

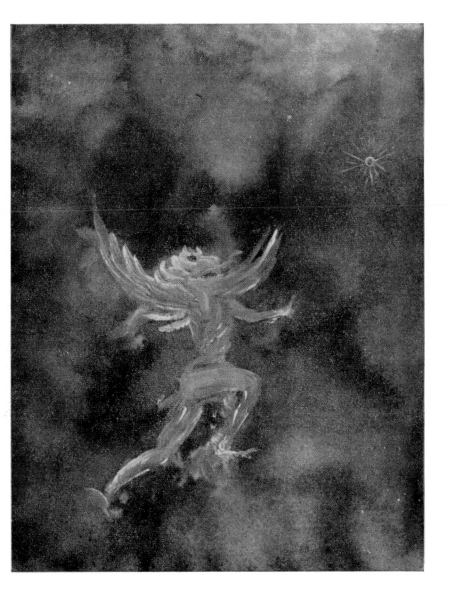

Figure 51

Figure 52

Figure 53

Figure 54

of the sun." Having reached that final goal, that safe resort, he now moves along the course of yonder sun.[17]

675   This sun has seven rays. A commentator remarks that four of them point to the four quarters; one points upwards, another downwards, but the seventh and "best" points inwards. It is at the same time the sun's disc, named Hiranyagarbha. This, according to Ramanuja's commentary on the Vedanta Sutras,[18] is the highest self, the "collective aggregate of all individual souls." It is the body of the highest Brahma and represents the collective psyche. For the idea of the self as compounded of many, compare Origen's "Each of us is not one, but many" and "All are righteous, but one receiveth the crown." [19]

676   The patient was a woman of sixty, artistically gifted. The individuation process, long blocked but released by the treatment, stimulated her creative activity (Fig. 21 derives from the same source) and gave rise to a series of happily coloured pictures which eloquently express the intensity of her experience.

Figure 24

677   Done by the same patient. She herself is shown practising contemplation or concentration on the centre: she has taken the place of the fish and the snakes. An ideal image of herself is laid round the precious egg. The legs are flexible, like a nixie's. The psychology of such a picture reappears in ecclesiastical tradition. The Shiva-Shakti of the East is known in the West as the "man encompassed by a woman," Christ and his bride the Church. Compare the Maitrayana-Brahmana Upanishad:

He [the Self] is also he who warms, the Sun, hidden by the thousand-eyed golden egg, as one fire by another. He is to be thought after, he is to be sought after. Having said farewell to all living things, having gone to the forest, and having renounced all sensuous objects, let a man perceive the Self from his own body.[20]

678   Here too the radiation from the centre spreads out beyond the protective circle into the distance. This expresses the idea of the far-reaching effect of the introverted state of conscious-

17 I, 9, 3, 15ff. Trans. from *Sacred Books of the East*, XII, pp. 271f., modified.
18 Trans. from *Sacred Books of the East*, XLVIII, p. 578.
19 *In libros Regnorum homiliae*, I, 4 (Migne, *P.G.*, vol. 12, cols. 998, 999).
20 VI, 8. Trans. from *Sacred Books of the East*, XV, p. 311.

ness. It could also be described as an *unconscious* connection with the world.

Figure 25

679   This picture was done by another middle-aged patient. It shows various phases of the individuation process. Down below she is caught in a chthonic tangle of roots (the *mūlādhāra* of *kundalini* yoga). In the middle she studies a book, cultivating her mind and augmenting her knowledge and consciousness. At the top, reborn, she receives illumination in the form of a heavenly sphere that widens and frees the personality, its round shape again representing the mandala in its "Kingdom of God" aspect, whereas the lower, wheel-shaped mandala is chthonic. There is a confrontation of the natural and spiritual totalities. The mandala is unusual on account of its six rays, six mountain peaks, six birds, three human figures. In addition, it is located between a distinct Above and Below, also repeated in the mandala itself. The upper, bright sphere is in the act of descending into the hexad or triad and has already passed the rim of the wheel. According to old tradition the number 6 means creation and evolution, since it is a *coniunctio* of 2 and 3 (even and odd = female and male). Philo Judaeus therefore calls the *senarius* (6) the "number most suited to generation." [21] The number 3, he says, denotes the surface or flatness, whereas 4 means height or depth. The *quaternarius* "shows the nature of solids," whereas the three first numbers characterize or produce incorporeal intelligences. The number 4 appears as a three-sided pyramid.[22] The hexad shows that the mandala consists of two triads, and the upper one is making itself into a quaternity, the state of "equability and justice," as Philo says. Down below lurk unintegrated dark clouds. This picture demonstrates the not uncommon fact that the personality needs to be extended both upwards and downwards.

Figures 26 and 27

680   These mandalas are in part atypical. Both were done by the same young woman. In the centre, as in the previous mandala, is a female figure, as if enclosed in a glass sphere or transparent

21 *De opificio mundi.* Cf. Colson trans., I, p. 13.   22 Ibid., p. 79.

bubble. It looks almost as if an homunculus were in the making. In addition to the usual four or eight rays, both mandalas show a pentadic element. There is thus a dilemma between four and five. Five is the number assigned to the "natural" man, in so far as he consists of a trunk with five appendages. Four, on the other hand, signifies a *conscious* totality. It describes the ideal, "spiritual" man and formulates him as a totality in contrast to the pentad, which describes the corporeal man. It is significant that the swastika symbolizes the "ideal" man,[23] whereas the five-pointed star symbolizes the material and bodily man.[24] The dilemma of four and five corresponds to the conflict between "culture" and "nature." That was the problem of the patient. In Figure 26 the dilemma is indicated by the four groups of stars: two of them contain four stars and two of them five stars. On the rims of both mandalas we see the "fire of desire." In Figure 27 the rim is made of something that looks like lighted tissue. In characteristic contrast to the "shining" mandala, both these (especially the second one) are "burning." It is flaming desire, comparable to the longing of the homunculus in the retort (*Faust*, Part II), which was finally shattered against the throne of Galatea. The fire represents an erotic demand but at the same time an *amor fati* that burns in the innermost self, trying to shape the patient's fate and thus help the self into reality. Like the homunculus in *Faust*, the figure shut up in the vessel wants to "become."

681   The patient was herself aware of the conflict, for she told me she had no peace after painting the second picture. She had reached the afternoon of her life, and was in her thirty-fifth year. She was in doubt as to whether she ought to have another child. She decided for a child, but fate did not let her, because the development of her personality was evidently pursuing a different goal, not a biological but a cultural one. The conflict was resolved in the interests of the latter.

23 It depends very much on whether the swastika revolves to the right or to the left. In Tibet, the one that revolves to the left is supposed to symbolize the Bŏn religion of black magic as opposed to Buddhism.
24 The symbol of the star is favoured both by Russia and America. The one is red, the other white. For the significance of these colours see *Psychology and Alchemy*, index, s.v. "colours."

Figure 28

682   Picture by a middle-aged man. In the centre is a star. The blue sky contains golden clouds. At the four cardinal points we see human figures: at the top, an old man in the attitude of contemplation; at the bottom, Loki or Hephaestus with red, flaming hair, holding in his hands a temple. To the right and left are a light and a dark female figure. Together they indicate four aspects of the personality, or four archetypal figures belonging, as it were, to the periphery of the self. The two female figures can be recognized without difficulty as the two aspects of the anima. The old man corresponds to the archetype of meaning, or of the spirit, and the dark chthonic figure to the opposite of the Wise Old Man, namely the magical (and sometimes destructive) Luciferian element. In alchemy it is Hermes Trismegistus versus Mercurius, the evasive "trickster." [25] The circle enclosing the sky contains structures or organisms that look like protozoa. The sixteen globes painted in four colours just outside this circle derived originally from an eye motif and therefore stand for the observing and discriminating consciousness. Similarly, the ornaments in the next circle, all opening inwards, are rather like vessels pouring out their content towards the centre.[26] On the other hand the ornaments along the rim open outwards, as if to receive something from outside. That is, in the individuation process what were originally projections stream back "inside" and are integrated into the personality again. Here, in contrast to Figure 25, "Above" and "Below," male and female, are integrated, as in the alchemical hermaphrodite.

Figure 29

683   Once again the centre is symbolized by a star. This very common image is consistent with the previous pictures, where the sun represents the centre. The sun, too, is a star, a radiant cell in the ocean of the sky. The picture shows the self appear-

25 Cf. the eighth and the ninth papers in this volume; and "The Spirit Mercurius."

26 There is a similar conception in alchemy, in the Ripley Scrowle and its variants (*Psychology and Alchemy*, fig. 257). There it is the planetary gods who are pouring their qualities into the bath of rebirth.

ing as a star out of chaos. The four-rayed structure is emphasized by the use of four colours. This picture is significant in that it sets the structure of the self as a principle of order against chaos.[27] It was painted by the same man who did Figure 28.

Figure 30

684   This mandala, by an older woman patient, is again split into Above and Below: heaven above, the sea below, as indicated by the golden waves on a green ground. Four wings revolve leftwards about the centre, which is marked only by an orange-red spot. Here too the opposites are integrated and are presumably the cause of the centre's rotation.

Figure 31

685   An atypical mandala, based on a dyad. A golden moon and a silver moon form the upper and lower edges. The inside is blue sky above and something like a black crenellated wall below. On it there sits a peacock, fanning out its tail, and to the left there is an egg, presumably the peacock's. In view of the important role which the peacock and the peacock's egg together play in alchemy and also in Gnosticism, we may expect the miracle of the *cauda pavonis,* the appearance of "all Colours" (Böhme), the unfolding and realization of wholeness, once the dark dividing wall has broken down. (See Fig. 32.) The patient thought the egg might split and produce something new, maybe a snake. In alchemy the peacock is synonymous with the Phoenix. A variant of the Phoenix legend relates that the Semenda Bird consumes itself, a worm forms from the ashes, and from the worm the bird rises anew.

Figure 32

686   This picture is reproduced from the Codex Alchemicus Rhenoviensis, Central Library, Zurich. Here the peacock represents the Phoenix rising newborn from the fire. There is a similar picture in a manuscript in the British Museum, only there the peacock is enclosed in a flask, the *vas hermeticum,* like the homunculus.[28] The peacock is an old emblem of rebirth and resurrection, quite frequently found on Christian

27 Cf. "The Psychology of Eastern Meditation," par. 942.
28 Cf. John Read, *Prelude to Chemistry,* frontispiece.

sarcophagi. In the vessel standing beside the peacock the colours of the *cauda pavonis* appear, as a sign that the transformation process is nearing its goal. In the alchemical process the *serpens mercurialis,* the dragon, is changed into the eagle, the peacock, the goose of Hermes, or the Phoenix.[29]

Figure 33

687   This picture was done by a seven-year-old boy, offspring of a problem marriage. He had done a whole series of these drawings of circles and hung them up round his bed. He called them his "loves" and would not go to sleep without them. This shows that the "magical" pictures still functioned for him in their original sense, as a protective magic circle.

Figure 34

688   An eleven-year-old girl, whose parents were divorced, had, at a time of great difficulties and upsets, drawn a number of pictures which clearly reveal a mandala structure. Here too they were magic circles intended to stop the difficulties and adversities of the outside world from entering into the inner psychic space. They represent a kind of self-protection.

689   As on the *kilkhor,* the Tibetan World Wheel (Fig. 3), you can see at either side of this picture something that looks like horns, which as we know belong to the devil or to one of his theriomorphic symbols. The slanting eye-slits underneath them, and the two strokes for nose and mouth, are also the devil's. This amounts to saying: Behind the mandala lurks the devil. Either the "demons" are covered up by the magically powerful picture, and thereby eliminated—which would be the purpose of the mandala—or, as in the case of the Tibetan World Wheel, the world is caught in the claws of the demon of death. In this picture the devils merely peek out over the edge. I have seen what this means from another case: An artistically gifted patient produced a typical tetradic mandala and stuck it on a sheet of thick paper. On the back there was a circle to match, filled with drawings of sexual perversions. This shadow aspect of the mandala represented the disorderly, disruptive tendencies, the "chaos" that hides behind the self and bursts out in a dan-

---

[29] Cf. *Psychology and Alchemy,* pars. 334 and 404.

gerous way as soon as the individuation process comes to a standstill, or when the self is not realized and so remains unconscious. This piece of psychology was expressed by the alchemists in their Mercurius duplex, who on the one hand is Hermes the mystagogue and psychopomp, and on the other hand is the poisonous dragon, the evil spirit and "trickster."

Figure 35

590   Drawing by the same girl. Round the sun is a circle with eyes, and round this an uroboros. The motif of polyophthalmia frequently occurs in individual mandalas. (See Picture 17 and Fig. 5 in the preceding paper.) In the Maitrayana-Brahmana Upanishad VI, 8 the egg (Hiranyagarbha) is described as "thousand-eyed." The eyes in the mandala no doubt signify the observing consciousness, but it must also be borne in mind that the texts as well as the pictures both attribute the eyes to a mythic figure, e.g., an Anthropos, who does the seeing. This seems to me to point to the fascination which, through a kind of magical stare, attracts the attention of the conscious mind. (Cf. Figs. 38 and 39.)

Figure 36

691   Painting of a medieval city with walls and moats, streets and churches, arranged quadratically. The inner city is again surrounded by walls and moats, like the Imperial City in Peking. The buildings all open inwards, towards the centre, represented by a castle with a golden roof. It too is surrounded by a moat. The ground round the castle is laid with black and white tiles, representing the united opposites. This mandala was done by a middle-aged man (cf. Figs. 6, 28, 29). A picture like this is not unknown in Christian symbolism. The Heavenly Jerusalem of Revelation is known to everybody. Coming to the Indian world of ideas, we find the city of Brahma on the world mountain, Meru. We read in the *Golden Flower*: "The *Book of the Yellow Castle* says: 'In the square inch field of the square foot house, life can be regulated.' The square foot house is the face. The square inch field in the face: what could that be other than the heavenly heart? In the middle of the square inch dwells the splendour. In the purple hall of

the city of jade dwells the God of Utmost Emptiness and life." [30]
ness and life." [30]

Figure 37

692   Painted by the same patient who did Figures 11 and 30. Here the "seeding-place" is depicted as a child enclosed in a revolving sphere. The four "wings" are painted in the four basic colours. The child corresponds to Hiranyagarbha and to the homunculus of the alchemists. The mythologem of the "Divine Child" is based on ideas of this sort.[31]

Figure 38

693   Mandala in rotation, by the same patient. who did Figures 21 and 23. A notable feature is the quaternary structure of the golden wings in combination with the triad of three dogs running round the centre. They have their backs to it, indicating that for them the centre is in the unconscious. The mandala contains—another unusual feature—a triadic motif turning to the left, while the wings turn to the right. This is not accidental. The dogs represent consciousness "scenting" or "intuiting" the unconscious; the wings show the movement of the unconscious towards consciousness, as corresponded to the patient's situation at the time. It is as if the dogs were fascinated by the centre although they cannot see it. They seem to represent the fascination felt by the conscious mind. The picture embodies the above-mentioned sesquitertian proportion (3 : 4).

Figure 39

694   The same motif as before, but represented by hares. From a Gothic window in the cathedral at Paderborn. There is no recognizable centre though the rotation presupposes one.

Figure 40

695   Picture by a young woman patient. It too exhibits the sesquitertian proportion and hence the dilemma with which Plato's *Timaeus* begins, and which as I said plays a considerable role in alchemy, as the axiom of Maria.[32]

[30] *The Secret of the Golden Flower* (1962), p. 22.
[31] Cf. Jung, "The Psychological Aspects of the Kore" and "The Psychology of the Child Archetype."
[32] Cf. "A Psychological Approach to the Dogma of the Trinity," par. 184.

Figure 41

96   This picture was done by a young woman patient with a schizoid disposition. The pathological element is revealed in the "breaking lines" that split up the centre. The sharp, pointed forms of these breaking lines indicate evil, hurtful, and destructive impulses which might hinder the desired synthesis of personality. But it seems as if the regular structure of the surrounding mandala might be able to restrain the dangerous tendencies to dissociation. And this proved to be the case in the further course of the treatment and subsequent development of the patient.

Figure 42

97   A neurotically disturbed mandala. It was drawn by a young, unmarried woman patient at a time that was full of conflict: she was in a dilemma between two men. The outer rim shows four different colours. The centre is doubled in a curious way: fire breaks out from behind the blue star in the black field, while to the right a sun appears, with blood vessels running through it. The five-pointed star suggests a pentagram symbolizing man, the arms, legs, and head all having the same value. As I have said, it signifies the purely instinctual, chthonic, unconscious man. (Cf. Figs. 26 and 27.) The colour of the star is blue—of a cool nature, therefore. But the nascent sun is yellow and red—a warm colour. The sun itself (looking rather like the yolk of an incubated egg) usually denotes consciousness, illumination, understanding. Hence we could say of this mandala: a light is gradually dawning on the patient, she is waking out of her formerly unconscious state, which corresponded to a purely biological and rational existence. (Rationalism is no guarantee of higher consciousness, but merely of a one-sided one!) The new state is characterized by red (feeling) and yellow or gold (intuition). There is thus a shifting of the centre of personality into the warmer region of heart and feeling, while the inclusion of intuition suggests a groping, irrational apprehension of wholeness.

Figure 43

698   This picture was done by a middle-aged woman who, without being neurotic, was struggling for spiritual development
and used for this purpose the method of active imagination.
These efforts induced her to make a drawing of the birth of a
new insight or conscious awareness (eye) from the depths of the
unconscious (sea). Here the eye signifies the self.

Figure 44

699   Drawing of motif from a Roman mosaic on the floor of a
house in Moknine, Tunis, which I photographed. It represents
an apotropaism against the evil eye.

Figure 45

700   Mandala from the Navaho Indians, who with great toil
prepare such mandalas from coloured sand for curative purposes. It is part of the Mountain Chant Rite performed for the
sick. Around the centre there runs, in a wide arc, the body of
the Rainbow Goddess. A square head denotes a female deity, a
round one a male deity. The arrangement of the four pairs of
deities on the arms of the cross suggests a swastika wheeling to
the right. The four male deities who surround the swastika are
making the same movement.

Figure 46

701   Another sand-painting by the Navahos, from the Male
Shooting Chant. The four horned heads are painted in the four
colours that correspond to the four directions.[33]

Figure 47

702   Here, for comparison, is a painting of the Egyptian Sky
Mother, bending, like the Rainbow Goddess, over the "Land"
with its round horizon. Behind the mandala stands—presumably—the Air God, like the demon in Figures 3 and 34. Underneath, the arms of the *ka,* raised in adoration and decked with

---

[33] I am indebted to Mrs. Margaret Schevill for both these pictures. Figure 45 is
a variant of the sand-painting reproduced in *Psychology and Alchemy,* fig. 110.

the eye motif, hold the mandala, which probably signifies the wholeness of the "Two Lands." [34]

Figure 48

703   This picture, from a manuscript of Hildegard of Bingen, shows the earth surrounded by the ocean, realm of air, and starry heaven. The actual globe of the earth in the centre is divided into four.[35]

704   Böhme has a mandala in his book *XL Questions concerning the Soule* (see Fig. 1 of preceding paper). The periphery contains a bright and a dark hemisphere turning their backs to one another. They represent un-united opposites, which presumably should be bound together by the heart standing between them. This drawing is most unusual, but aptly expresses the insoluble moral conflict underlying the Christian view of the world. "The Soul," Böhme says, "is an Eye in the Eternal Abyss, a similitude of Eternity, a perfect Figure and Image of the first Principle, and resembles God the Father in his Person, as to the eternal Nature. The Essence and Substance of it, merely as to what it is purely in itself, is first the wheel of Nature, with the first four Forms." In the same treatise Böhme says: "The substance and Image of the soul may be resembled to the Earth, having a fair flower growing out of it . . ." "The Soul is a fiery Eye . . . from the eternal Centre of Nature . . . a similitude of the First Principle." [36] As an eye, the soul "receives the Light, as the Moon does the glance of the Sun . . . for the life of the soul has its original in the Fire." [37]

Figures 49 and 50

705   Figure 49 is especially interesting because it shows us very clearly in what relationship the picture stands to the painter. The patient (the same as did Fig. 42) has a shadow problem. The female figure in the picture represents her dark, chthonic side. She is standing in front of a wheel with four spokes, the two together forming an eight-rayed mandala. From her head

---

[34] The drawing was sent to me from the British Museum, London. The original painting appears to be in New York.
[35] Lucca, Bibliotheca governativa, Cod. 1942, fol. 37ʳ.
[36] *A Summary Appendix of the Soul*, p. 117.
[37] Ibid., p. 118.

spring four snakes,[38] expressing the tetradic nature of conscious-ness, but—in accordance with the demonic character of the pic-ture—they do this in an evil and nefarious way, since they represent evil and destructive thoughts. The entire figure is wrapped in flames, emitting a dazzling light. She is like a fiery demon, a salamander, the medieval conception of a fire sprite. Fire expresses an intense transformation process. Hence the *prima materia* in alchemy was symbolized by the salamander in the fire, as the next picture shows.[39] The spear- or arrow-head expresses "direction": it is pointing upwards from the middle of the head. Everything that the fire consumes rises up to the seat of the gods. The dragon glowing in the fire becomes volatil-ized; illumination comes through the fiery torment. Figure 49 tells us something about the background of the transformation process. It depicts a state of suffering, reminiscent on the one hand of crucifixion and on the other of Ixion bound to the wheel. From this it is evident that individuation, or becoming whole, is neither a *summum bonum* nor a *summum desider-atum,* but the painful experience of the union of opposites. That is the real meaning of the cross in the circle, and that is why the cross has an apotropaic effect, because, pointed at evil, it shows evil that it is already included and has therefore lost its destructive power.

Figure 51

706   This picture was done by a sixty-year-old woman patient with a similar problem: A fiery demon mounts through the night towards a star. There he passes over from a chaotic into an ordered and fixed state. The star stands for the transcendent totality, the demon for the animus, who, like the anima, is the connecting link between conscious and unconscious. The pic-ture recalls the antique symbolism found, for instance, in Plutarch: [40] The soul is only partly in the body, the other part is outside it and soars above man like a star symbolizing his "genius." The same conception can be found among the al-chemists.

[38] Cf. the four snakes in the chthonic, shadow-half of Picture 9 in the preceding paper.
[39] Figure X from Lambspringk's Symbols in the *Musaeum hermeticum* (Waite trans., I, p. 295).   [40] *De genio Socratis,* cap. XXII.

Figure 52

707   Picture by the same patient as before, showing flames with a soul rising up from them, as if swimming. The motif is repeated in Figure 53. Exactly the same thing—and with the same meaning—can be found in the Codex Rhenoviensis (fifteenth century), Zurich (Fig. 54). The souls of the calcined *prima materia* escape as vapours, in the form of human figures looking like children (homunculi). In the fire is the dragon, the chthonic form of the *anima mundi,* which is being transmuted.

Figures 53 and 54

708   Here I must remark that not only did the patient have no knowledge of alchemy but that I myself knew nothing at that time of the alchemical picture material. The resemblance between these two pictures, striking as it is, is nothing extraordinary, since the great problem and concern of philosophical alchemy was the same as underlies the psychology of the unconscious, namely individuation, the integration of the self. Similar causes (other things being equal) have similar effects, and similar psychological situations make use of the same symbols, which on their side rest on archetypal foundations, as I have shown in the case of alchemy.

Conclusion

709   I hope I have succeeded in giving the reader some idea of mandala symbolism with the help of these pictures. Naturally my exposition aims at nothing more than a superficial survey of the empirical material on which comparative research is based. I have indicated a few parallels that may point the way to further historical and ethnic comparisons, but have refrained from a more complete and more thorough exposition because it would have taken me too far.

710   I need say only a few words about the functional significance of the mandala, as I have discussed this theme several times before. Moreover, if we have a little feeling in our fingertips we can guess from these pictures, painted with the greatest devotion but with unskilful hands, what is the deeper meaning that the patients tried to put into them and express through them. They are *yantras* in the Indian sense, instruments of meditation,

concentration, and self-immersion, for the purpose of realizing inner experience, as I have explained in the commentary to the *Golden Flower*. At the same time they serve to produce an inner order—which is why, when they appear in a series, they often follow chaotic, disordered states marked by conflict and anxiety. They express the idea of a safe refuge, of inner reconciliation and wholeness.

711 I could produce many more pictures from all parts of the world, and one would be astonished to see how these symbols are governed by the same fundamental laws that can be observed in individual mandalas. In view of the fact that all the mandalas shown here were new and uninfluenced products, we are driven to the conclusion that there must be a transconscious disposition in every individual which is able to produce the same or very similar symbols at all times and in all places. Since this disposition is usually not a conscious possession of the individual I have called it the *collective unconscious,* and, as the bases of its symbolical products, I postulate the existence of primordial images, the *archetypes*. I need hardly add that the identity of unconscious individual contents with their ethnic parallels is expressed not merely in their form but in their meaning.

712 Knowledge of the common origin of these unconsciously preformed symbols has been totally lost to us. In order to recover it, we have to read old texts and investigate old cultures, so as to gain an understanding of the things our patients bring us today in explanation of their psychic development. And when we penetrate a little more deeply below the surface of the psyche, we come upon historical layers which are not just dead dust, but alive and continuously active in everyone—maybe to a degree that we cannot imagine in the present state of our knowledge.

BIBLIOGRAPHY

ADLER, GERHARD. *Studies in Analytical Psychology*. London, 1948; 2nd edn., London, 1966, New York, 1967.

AETIUS. *De placitis philosophorum reliquiae*. In: HERMANN DIELS (ed.). *Doxographi Graeci*. Berlin, 1879.

Amitāyur-dhyāna Sūtra. In: *Buddhist Mahāyāna Sūtras*, Part II. Translated by F. Max Müller and Junjiro Takakusu. (Sacred Books of the East, 49.) Oxford, 1894.

APTOWITZER, VICTOR. "Arabisch-Jüdische Schöpfungstheorien," *Hebrew Union College Annual* (Cincinnati), VI (1929).

APULEIUS, LUCIUS. *The Golden Ass*. Translated by Robert Graves. (Penguin Classics.) Harmondsworth, 1954.

BÄNZIGER, HANS. "Persönliches und Archetypisches in Individuationsprozess," *Schweizerische Zeitschrift für Psychologie und ihre Anwendungen* (Bern), VI (1947), 272–83.

BAUMGARTNER, MATHIAS. *Die Philosophie des Alanus de Insulis*. (Beiträge zur Geschichte der Philosophie des Mittelalters, 2:4.) Munster, 1896.

BERTHELOT, MARCELLIN. *La Chimie au moyen âge*. Paris, 1893. 3 vols.

———. *Collection des anciens alchimistes grecs*. Paris, 1887–88. 3 vols.

[BÖHME, JAKOB.] *XL Questions concerning the Soule, propounded by Dr. Balthasar Walter and answered by Jacob Behmen*. London, 1647.

———. *Des gottseligen hocherleuchteten Jacob Böhmen Teutonici Philosophi Alle Theosophische Schrifften*. Amsterdam, 1682. (This edition of Böhme's works consists of a number of parts, each separately paginated and variously bound up. The parts are not numbered. It includes, *inter alia*, the following works referred to in the present volume. The bracketed English titles and volume references following the German title of each work refer to the 1764–81 London translation cited below.)

Aurora. Morgenröte im Ausgang . . . [*Aurora:* Vol. I.]

[*Drey principia.*] *Beschreibung der drey Principien Göttliches Wesens.* [*Three Principles of the Divine Essence:* Vol. I.]

Hohe und tiefe Gründe von dem dreyfachen Leben des Menschen. [*The High and Deep Searching of the Three-fold Life of Man:* Vol. II.]

Signatura rerum. [*Signatura rerum:* Vol. IV.]

Tabulae principiorum. [*Four Tables of Divine Revelation:* Vol. III.]

[*Quaestiones Theosophicae.*] *Theosophische Fragen in Betrachtung Göttliche Offenbharung* . . . [Not included in English collection.]

Vierzig Fragen von der Seelen Urstand . . . *verfasset von Dr. Balthasar Walter und beantwortet durch Jacob Böhme.* [*Forty Questions concerning the Soul:* Vol. II.]

Die Umgewandte Auge. [*A Summary Appendix of the Soul:* Vol. II.]

————. *Mysterium pansophicum, oder Gründliche Bericht vom irdischen und himmlischen Mysterio.* In: *Jakob Böhme's sämtliche Werke.* Edited by K. W. Schiebler. Leipzig, 1831–46. 6 vols. (Vol. 6, pp. 411–24.)

————. *The Works of Jacob Behmen.* [Edited by G. Ward and T. Langcake.] London, 1764–81. 4 vols.

Bouché-Leclercq, Auguste. *L'Astrologie grecque.* Paris, 1899.

Bozzano, Ernesto. *Popoli primitivi Manifestazioni supernormali.* Verona, 1941.

Caesarius of Heisterbach. *The Dialogue on Miracles.* Translated by H. von E. Scott and C. C. Swinton Bland. London, 1929. 2 vols. (Original: *Dialogus Miraculorum.* Edited by J. Strange, 1851.)

Caussin, Nicholas. *De symbolica Aegyptiorum sapientia. Polyhistor symbolicus, Electorum symbolorum, & Parabolarum historicarum stromata.* Paris, [1618 and] 1631.

CHARLES, ROBERT HENRY (ed.). *The Apocrypha and Pseudepigrapha of the Old Testament in English.* Oxford, 1913. 2 vols.

CICERO, MARCUS TULLIUS. *De natura deorum: Academica.* With an English text by H. Rackham. (Loeb Classical Library.) London and New York, 1933.

CLEMENT OF ALEXANDRIA. *Stromata.* In: CLEMENS ALEXANDRINUS. *Werke,* Vol. II. Edited by Otto Stählin. (Griechische christliche Schriftsteller.) Leipzig, 1906. For translation see: *The Writings of Clement of Alexandria.* Translated by William Wilson. (Ante-Nicene Christian Library, 4, 12.) Edinburgh, 1867, 1869. 2 vols.

CUMONT, FRANZ. *Textes et monuments figurés relatifs aux mystères de Mithra.* Brussels, 1894–99. 2 vols.

DEE, JOHN. "Monas hieroglyphica." See *Theatrum chemicum.*

DE GUBERNATIS, ANGELO. *Zoological Mythology.* London, 1872. 2 vols.

DELATTE, LOUIS (ed.). *Textes latins et vieux français relatifs aux Cyranides.* (Bibliothèque de la Faculté de Philosophie et Lettres d l'Université de Liège, fasc. 93.) Liège and Paris, 1942.

DEUSSEN, PAUL. *Allgemeine Geschichte der Philosophie.* Leipzig, 1894–1917. 2 vols.

DIELS, HERMANN. *Fragmente der Vorsokratiker.* 5th edn., Berlin, 1934–37. 3 vols.

DORN, GERHARD (Gerardus Dorneus). See *Theatrum chemicum.*

EISLER, ROBERT. *Weltenmantel und Himmelszelt.* Munich, 1910. 2 vols.

ELEAZAR, R. ABRAHAM. *Uraltes Chymisches Werk.* Leipzig, 1760.

ERMAN, ADOLF. *Handbook of Egyptian Religion.* London, 1907.

———. *Die Religion der Agypter.* Berlin and Leipzig, 1934.

FREEMAN, KATHLEEN. *Ancilla to the Pre-Socratic Philosophers.* Oxford, 1948.

FROBENIUS, LEO. *Schicksalskunde.* (Schriften zur Schicksalskunde, 5.) Weimar, 1938.

GESSMANN, GUSTAV WILHELM. *Die Geheimsymbole der Alchymie, Arzneikunde und Astrologie des Mittelalters.* 2nd edn., Berlin, 1922.

GLAUBER, JOHANN RUDOLPH. *Tractatus de natura salium.* Amsterdam, 1658. 2 parts.

HARDING, M. ESTHER. *Psychic Energy: Its Source and Goal.* (Bollingen Series X.) New York, 1948; 2nd edn., 1963: *Psychic Energy: Its Source and Its Transformation.*

HAUCK, ALBERT (ed.). *Real-encyclopädie für protestantische Theologie und Kirche.* Leipzig, 1896–1913. 24 vols.

HILDEGARDE OF BINGEN, SAINT. "Liber divinorum operum." Biblioteca governativa, Lucca, Codex 1942.

HIPPOLYTUS. *Elenchos (Refutatio omnium haeresium).* In: *Hippolytus' Werke.* Edited by Paul Wendland. (Griechische christliche Schriftsteller.) Vol. III. Leipzig, 1916. For translation, see: *Philosophumena: or, The Refutation of all Heresies.* Translated by Francis Legge. London and New York, 1921. 2 vols.

HOFFMANN-KRAYER, E., and BÄCHTOLD-STÄUBLI, HANNS. *Handwörterbuch des deutschen Aberglaubens.* (Handwörterbucher für deutschen Volkskünde, Abt. I.) Berlin and Leipzig, 1927–37. 8 vols.

HORAPOLLO NILIACUS. *Hieroglyphica.* See: *The Hieroglyphics of Horapollo.* Translated by George Boas. (Bollingen Series XXIII.) New York, 1950. (Original: *Selecta Hieroglyphica.* Rome, 1597.)

I Ching, or Book of Changes. The German translation by Richard Wilhelm, rendered into English by Cary F. Baynes. New York (Bollingen Series XIX) and London, 1950; 3rd edn., 1967.

JACOBI, JOLANDE. *Complex/Archetype/Symbol in the Psychology of C. G. Jung.* Translated by Ralph Manheim. New York (Bollingen Series) and London, 1959. (Also a P/B.)*

JEROME, SAINT. *Epistola II ad Theodosium et ceteros Anachoretas.* In: *Hieronymi Epistularum Pars I.* (Corpus Scriptorum Ecclesiasticorum Latinorum, 54.) Vienna and Leipzig, 1910.

* P/B = Princeton/Bollingen Paperback.

JUNG, CARL GUSTAV. "The Aims of Psychotherapy." In: *The Practice of Psychotherapy. Collected Works,** Vol. 16. New York and London, 2nd edn., 1966.

———. *Aion: Researches into the Phenomenology of the Self. Collected Works,** Vol. 9, Part II. Princeton and London, 2nd edn., 1968.

———. *Alchemical Studies. Collected Works,** Vol. 13. Princeton and London, 1968.

———. "Answer to Job." In: *Psychology and Religion: West and East,* q.v.

———. *The Archetypes and the Collective Unconscious. Collected Works,** Vol. 9, Part I. Princeton and London, 2nd edn., 1968.

———. *Collected Papers on Analytical Psychology.* Edited by Constance Long. 2nd edn., London, 1917; New York, 1920.

———. Commentary on "The Secret of the Golden Flower." In: *Alchemical Studies.* (See also WILHELM and JUNG, *The Secret of the Golden Flower.*)

———. *Memories, Dreams, Reflections.* Recorded and edited by Aniela Jaffé. Translated by Richard and Clara Winston. New York and London, 1963. (U.S. and Brit. edns. separately paginated.)

———. "On the Nature of the Psyche." In: *The Structure and Dynamics of the Psyche,* q.v. (Also a P/B.)

———. "Paracelsus as a Spiritual Phenomenon." In: *Alchemical Studies,* q.v.

———. "The Phenomenology of the Spirit in Fairytales." In: *The Archetypes and the Collective Unconscious,* q.v.

———. "The Philosophical Tree." In: *Alchemical Studies,* q.v.

———. *The Practice of Psychotherapy. Collected Works,** Vol. 16. New York and London, 2nd edn., 1966.

* For details of the *Collected Works of C. G. Jung,* see end of this volume.

———. "A Psychological Approach to the Dogma of the Trinity." In: *Psychology and Religion: West and East,* q.v.

———. "The Psychological Aspects of the Kore" and "The Psychology of the Child Archetype." In: C. KERÉNYI and C. G. JUNG. *Essays on a Science of Mythology.* (Bollingen Series XXII.) New York, 1949. (Also a P/B.)

———. Psychological Commentary on "The Tibetan Book of the Dead." In: ibid.

———. *Psychological Types. Collected Works,** Vol. 6. Princeton and London, 1971.

———. *Psychology and Alchemy. Collected Works,** Vol. 12. Princeton and London, 2nd edn., 1968.

———. "The Psychology of Eastern Meditation." In: *Psychology and Religion: West and East,* q.v.

———. *Psychology and Religion: West and East. Collected Works,** Vol. 11. New York and London, 1958.

———. "The Psychology of the Transference." In: *The Practice of Psychotherapy,* q.v. (Also a P/B.)

———. "The Relations between the Ego and the Unconscious." In: *Two Essays on Analytical Psychology,* q.v.

———. "The Spirit Mercurius." In: *Alchemical Studies,* q.v.

———. *Symbols of Transformation. Collected Works,** Vol. 5. Princeton and London, 2nd edn., 1967.

———. "Synchronicity: An Acausal Connecting Phenomenon." In: *The Structure and Dynamics of the Psyche,* q.v.

———. "The Transcendent Function." In: ibid.

———. *Two Essays on Analytical Psychology. Collected Works,** Vol. 7. New York and London, 2nd edn., 1966. (Also a P/B.)

Kabbala Denudata. See KNORR VON ROSENROTH.

* For details of the *Collected Works of C. G. Jung,* see end of this volume.

KERÉNYI, KARL. "Hermes der Seelenführer," *Eranos Jahrbuch 1942* (Zurich, 1943), 9–107.

KHUNRATH, HENRICUS. *Von hylealischen, das ist, pri-materialischen . . . Chaos.* Magdeburg, 1597.

KNORR VON ROSENROTH, CHRISTIAN. *Kabbala Denudata.* Sulzbach, 1677–78 (Vol. I); Frankfurt a. M., 1684 (Vol. II). 2 vols. (*Adumbratio Kabbalae Christianae* is an appendix to Vol. II.) For partial translation, see: S. LIDELL MACGREGOR MATHERS. *The Kabbalah Unveiled.* London, 1887.

LACTANTIUS FIRMIANUS. *Divinae institutiones.* In: *Opera omnia.* Edited by Samuel Brandt and Georg Laubmann. (Corpus scriptorum ecclesiasticorum Latinorum.) Vienna, 1890–97. 3 vols. Vol. I. For translation, see: *The Works of Lactantius.* Translated by William Fletcher. (Ante-Nicene Christian Library, 21, 22.) Edinburgh, 1871. 2 vols.

LAMBSPRINGK. See WAITE.

LENGLET DU FRESNOY, PIERRE NICOLAS. *Histoire de la philosophie hermétique.* 1742. 3 vols.

LEONE EBREO (Leo Hebraeus) (Don Judah Abarbanel). *The Philosophy of Love.* Translated by F. Friedeberg-Seeley and Jean H. Barnes. London, 1937.

LÜDY, F. *Alchemistische und Chemische Zeichen.* Berlin, 1929.

MAIER, MICHAEL. *De circulo physico quadrato.* Oppenheim, 1616.

———. *Symbola aureae mensae duodecim nationum.* Frankfurt a. M., 1617.

Majjhima-Nikaya. See BHIKKHU SILACARA (ed. and trans.). *The First Fifty Discourses from the Collection of the Middle-Length Discourses (Majjhima Nikaya) of Gotama the Buddha.* Breslau and Leipzig, 1912–13. 2 vols.

MANGETUS, JOANNES JACOBUS (ed.). *BIBLIOTHECA CHEMICA CURIOSA, seu Rerum ad alchemiam pertinentium thesaurus instructissimus . . .* Coloniae Allobrogum [Geneva], 1702, 2 vols.

MASENIUS, JACOBUS. *Speculum imaginum veritatis occultae.* Cologne, 1714. 2 vols.

MEIER, C. A. *Ancient Incubation and Modern Psychotherapy.* Translated by Monica Curtis. Evanston, 1967.

———. "Spontanmanifestationen des kollektiven Unbewussten," *Zentralblatt für Psychotherapie* (Leipzig), XI (1939), 284ff.

MENNENS, GULIELMUS. *Aurei velleris, sive sacrae philosophiae, naturae et artis admirabilium libri tres.* Antwerp, 1604. See also "De aureo vellere" in *Theatrum chemicum.*

MIGNE, JACQUES PAUL (ed.). *Patrologiae cursus completus.* [*P. G.*] Greek series, Paris, 1857–66. 166 vols.

MYLIUS, JOHANN DANIEL. *Philosophia reformata.* Frankfurt a. M., 1622.

Mythographus Vaticanus III. See: *Classicorum Auctorum e Vaticanis Codicibus Editorum,* Vol. 6: *Complectens Mythographi tres.* Edited by Angelo Mai. Rome, 1831.

NEUMANN, ERICH. *Depth Psychology and a New Ethic.* Translated by Eugene Rolfe. New York and London, 1969.

NEWCOMB, FRANC JOHNSON, and REICHARD, GLADYS A. *Sand-paintings of the Navajo Shooting Chant.* New York, 1938.

[Panchatantra.] *The Panchatantra Reconstructed.* By Franklin Edgerton. (American Oriental Series, 2, 3.) New Haven, 1924. 2 vols.

PHILO JUDAEUS. *De opificio mundi.* In: *Philo.* With an English translation by Francis Henry Colson and George Herbert Whitaker. (Loeb Classical Library.) London and New York, 1929– . 12 vols. published. (Vol. I.)

PICINELLI, FILIPPO. *Mondo simbolico.* Milan, 1669. Translated into Latin as: *Mundus symbolicus.* Cologne, 1680–81.

PLATO. *The Symposium.* Translated by W. Hamilton. (Penguin Classics.) Harmondsworth, 1959.

———. *The Timaeus and the Critias.* The Thomas Taylor translation. (Bollingen Series III.) New York, 1944.

PLINY. [*Historia naturalis.*] *Natural History.* With an English translation by H. Rackham. (Loeb Classical Library.) London and New York, 1938– . 10 vols. published.

PLUTARCH. *De genio Socratis.* In: *Moralia.* Edited by C. Hubert et al. Leipzig, 1892–1935. 7 vols. (Vol. III, pp. 460–511.)

PREISENDANZ, KARL. *Papyri Graecae magicae.* Leipzig and Berlin, 1928–31. 2 vols.

[PROPERTIUS, SEXTUS.] *Propertius.* With an English translation by H. E. Butler. (Loeb Classical Library.) London and New York, 1912.

RAHNER, HUGO. "Antenna Crucis II: Das Meer der Welt," *Zeitschrift für Katholische Theologie* (Innsbruck), LXVI (1942), 89ff.

———. "Die seelenheilende Blume," *Eranos Jahrbuch* (Zurich), XII (C. G. Jung Festgabe, 1945), 117–239.

READ, JOHN. *Prelude to Chemistry.* London, 1939.

REUSNER, HIERONYMUS. *Pandora: das ist, die edelst Gab Gottes, oder der Werde und heilsame Stein der Weysen.* Basel, 1588.

Rig-Veda. See: *Hindu Scriptures.* Edited by Nicol MacNicol. (Everyman's Library.) London and New York, 1938. See also DEUSSEN.

ROSCHER, WILHELM HEINRICH. *Ausführliches Lexikon der Griechische und Römische Mythologie.* Leipzig, 1884–1937. 6 vols.

ROSENCREUTZ, CHRISTIAN. *Chymische Hochzeit.* Strasbourg, 1616. For translation, see: *The Hermetick Romance; or, The Chemical Wedding.* Translated by E. Foxcroft. London, 1690.

RULAND, MARTIN. *A Lexicon of Alchemy.* [London, 1893.] (Original: *Lexicon alchemiae.* Frankfurt a. M., 1612.)

Samyutta-Nikaya. See: *The Book of the Kindred Sayings (Sangyutta-Nikaya).* Part II: *The Nidana Book (Nidana-Vagga).* Translated by Mrs. C. A. F. Rhys Davids. London, [1922]. Also: *Dialogues of the Buddha.* Part II. Translated by T. W. and C. A. F. Rhys Davids. (Sacred Books of the Buddhists, 3.) London, 1951.

Sanatsugatiya. See: *The Bhagavadgita, with the Sanatsugatiya and the Anugita.* Translated by Kashinath Trimbak Telang. (Sacred Books of the East, 8.) Oxford, 1882.

SENDIVOGIUS, MICHAEL (Micha Sedziwoj). "Epistola XIII." See MANGETUS, *Bibliotheca chemica curiosa.*

STADE, BERNHARD. *Biblische Theologie des Alten Testaments.* Vol. I (no more published). Tübingen, 1905.

SUZUKI, DAISETZ TEITARO. *An Introduction to Zen Buddhism.* London, [1948].

THEATRUM CHEMICUM, praecipuos selectorum auctorum tractatus . . . continens. Ursellis [Ursel] and Argentorati [Strasbourg], 1602–61. 6 vols. (Vols. I-III, Ursel, 1602; Vols. IV–VI, Strasbourg, 1613, 1622, 1661 respectively.)

WAITE, ARTHUR EDWARD (ed. and trans.). *The Hermetic Museum Restored and Enlarged.* London, 1953. 2 vols. (The Book of Lambspring, I, pp. 271–306.)

[WEI PO-YANG.] "An Ancient Chinese Treatise on Alchemy entitled Ts'an T'ung Ch'i, written by Wei Po-yang about 142 A.D." Translated by Lu-ch'iang Wu and Tenney L. Davis. In: *Isis* (Bruges), XVIII (1932), 210–89.

WILHELM, RICHARD, and JUNG, CARL GUSTAV. *The Secret of the Golden Flower.* Translated by Cary F. Baynes. London and New York, 1931; revised edition, 1962.

INDEX

A

Abarbanel/Abrabanel, Judah, *see* Leone Ebreo

Abercius inscription, 26n

Achurayim, 14n, 44, 45f, 51

Adam, 33; Belial, 44n; First, 54n

Adler, Gerhard, 68n

Aeons, 11n, 26, 35, 44n

Aetius, 41n

agathodaimon, 33

Ain-Soph, 44n

Air God, 96

alchemists/alchemy, 21, 28, 44, 82, 91, 98; Böhme and, 57; Chinese, 9, 74; hermaphrodite/androgyny in, 100; lightning in, 11; mandalas in, 3; and Mercury/Mercurius, 30, 33

Alexander the Great, 59

America, 89n

amethysts, 16

Amitāyur-dhyāna Sūtra, 43n, 60n

angel(s): "fatherly" and "motherly," 26f, 33, 40; twelve wicked, 40

anima, 33, 36n, 73, 90, 98; as *ligamentum corporis et spiritus*, 29

Anima Christi, 44n

anima mundi, 28, 99

animal(s), in mandala, 82; *see also* beetle; birds; bull; crab; crayfish; crocodile; crow; dog; dove; eagle; falcon; fish; goat; goose; hare; lion; octopus; peacock; pig; raven; serpent; sheep; snake; swan; tortoise; worm

animus, 6f, 22, 33, 34, 49, 52, 73, 98; danger from, 60n; represented

by quicksilver, 28

anthracites, 16

anthrax, 16n, 47n

Anthropos, 9, 10, 20, 24, 28, 29, 82, 93

antimony, 17

Aphrodite, 43

Aptowitzer, Victor, 47n

Apuleius, 66

arbor philosophica, 49; *see also* tree, "philosophical"

archetype(s), 3, 73, 100, *etc.*; identification with, 67; of wholeness, 4; *see also* anima; animus; child; father; maiden; self; shadow; wise old man

arrows, 84f; arrow-head, 98

Artis auriferae, 47n

Asklepios, 27

Assumption, *see* Mary, the Virgin

astrology, 26, 59, 60n

Atman, 41

aurum philosophicum/ potabile/vitreum, 21; *see also* gold, philosophical

avatars, 26

B

ball, golden, 86

Bänziger, Hans, 68n

Barbelo-Gnosis, 35

Baruch, angel, 33, 40

Baruch, Apocalypse of, 11n

Basilides, 47n

Baumgartner, Matthias, 41n

bed, 49

Hercules Morbicida, 17n
hermaphrodite, 90
Hermes, 22, 23n, 27, 28, 93; ithyphallic, 30; Kyllenios, 11, 18
Hermes Trismegistus, 27, 90
hero(es), sun as/solar, 59n
hexad, 88
hierogamy, of sun and moon, 30n
hieroglyph, 18
Hildegard of Bingen, St., 97
Hīnayāna Buddhism, 74·
Hinduism, 26
Hippolytus, 11n, 18n, 27n, 33n, 40, 47
Hiranyagarbha, 84, 86, 87, 93, 94
Hölderlin, Friedrich, 45
Holy Ghost, 12
Homer: Odyssey, 18
homo: altus/interior/maximus, 24n, 28, 30; *quadratus*, 23
homunculus(-i), 9, 20, 31, 89, 91, 94, 99
Horapollo, 27n
horns, 69, 92
horoscope, 60
Horus, -child, 44, 79n, 83; four sons of, 4, 35, 62n, 82
hun (spirit), 36n

I

Ialdabaoth, 14n
Iamblichus, 42
I Ching, 55n, 58, 74, 75
Ichthys, 86; *see also* fish
icons, 77
identification, with archetype, 67
imagination, active, 8, 48, 67, 68, 71, 96
Imago Dei, 70; *see also* God-image
Indian philosophy, 5
individuation, 6f, 64, 66, 69ff, 87ff; analogy of creation, 24; *opus* as, 40
inflation, 67
instinct(s), 4, 19

intuition, 19
Iris, 46n
Isaiah, Book of, 66n
Isis, mysteries of, 66
"isms," 65
Ixion, 98

J

Jacobi, Jolande, 69n
Jerome, St., 32n
Jerusalem, heavenly, 93
Jesus, 33; *see also* Christ
Job, 35
John, St. (Evangelist), 15, 16
John of the Cross, St., 35n
Jung, Carl Gustav:
paintings by vi, ix (*frontisp.*), 80 (*Fig. 6*), 90 (*Figs. 28, 29*), 93 (*Fig. 36*)
CASES IN SUMMARY (*in order of presentation, numbered for reference*):
[1] American lady in psychic impasse: active imagination expressed in paintings. — 6ff
[2] Woman fond of playing with forms. — 63
See also 78–99; *many of the mandala pictures are from cases*
WORKS: "Aims of Psychotherapy, The," 68n; *Aion*, 23n, 26n, 83n, 86n; "Answer to Job," 44n; *Collected Papers on Analytical Psychology*, 22n; Commentary on *The Secret of the Golden Flower*, 36n, 68, 100; *Memories, Dreams, Reflections*, ix, 71n, 80n; "On the Nature of the Psyche," 30n, 62n; "Paracelsus as a Spiritual Phenomenon," 11n, 33n; "Philosophical Tree, The," 49n, 82n; *Practice of Psychotherapy, The*, 81n; "Psychological Approach to the Dogma of the Trinity, A," 39n,

THE COLLECTED WORKS OF
C. G. JUNG

THE PUBLICATION of the first complete edition, in English, of the works of C. G. Jung was undertaken by Routledge and Kegan Paul, Ltd., in England and by Bollingen Foundation in the United States. The American edition is number XX in Bollingen Series, which since 1967 has been published by Princeton University Press. The edition contains revised versions of works previously published, such as *Psychology of the Unconscious*, which is now entitled *Symbols of Transformation*; works originally written in English, such as *Psychology and Religion*; works not previously translated, such as *Aion*; and, in general, new translations of virtually all of Professor Jung's writings. Prior to his death, in 1961, the author supervised the textual revision, which in some cases is extensive. Sir Herbert Read (d. 1968), Dr. Michael Fordham, and Dr. Gerhard Adler compose the Editorial Committee; the translator is R. F. C. Hull (except for Volume 2) and William McGuire is executive editor.

The price of the volumes varies according to size; they are sold separately, and may also be obtained on standing order. Several of the volumes are extensively illustrated. Each volume contains an index and in most a bibliography; the final volume will contain a complete bibliography of Professor Jung's writings and a general index to the entire edition.

In the following list, dates of original publication are given in parentheses (of original composition, in brackets). Multiple dates indicate revisions.

(continued)

* Published 1960.   † Published 1961.
‡ Published 1956; 2nd edn., 1967. (65 plates, 43 text figures.)

* Published 1971.   † Published 1953; 2nd edn., 1966.
‡ Published 1960; 2nd edn., 1969.

* Published 1959; 2nd edn., 1968. (Part I: 79 plates, with 29 in colour.)

* Published 1964; 2nd edn., 1970. (8 plates.)
† Published 1958; 2nd edn., 1969.

* Published 1953; 2nd edn., completely revised, 1968. (270 illustrations.)
† Published 1968. (50 plates, 4 text figures.)
‡ Published 1963; 2nd edn., 1970. (10 plates.)

* Published 1966.
† Published 1954; 2nd edn., revised and augmented, 1966. (13 illustrations.)
‡ Published 1954.

The Development of Personality (1934)
Marriage as a Psychological Relationship (1925)

18. MISCELLANY
Posthumous and Other Miscellaneous Works

19. BIBLIOGRAPHY AND INDEX
Complete Bibliography of C. G. Jung's Writings
General Index to the Collected Works

Also available in Princeton/Bollingen Paperbacks: